The New Supervisor

Stepping Up with Confidence

Fourth Edition

Elwood N. Chapman and Wil McKnight

A Fifty-Minute™ Series Book

The New Supervisor

Stepping Up with Confidence

Fourth Edition

**Elwood N. Chapman and
Wil McKnight**

CREDITS:
Senior Editor: **Debbie Woodbury**
Editor: **Ann Gosch**
Assistant Editor: **Genevieve Del Rosario**
Production Manager: **Judy Petry**
Design: **Nicole Phillips**
Production Artist: **Rich Lehl**
Cartoonist: **Ralph Mapson**

© 1986 1988, 1992, 2003 Crisp Publications, Inc.
Printed in the United States of America by Von Hoffmann Graphics, Inc.

www.crisplearning.com

03 04 05 06   10 9 8 7 6 5 4 3 2 1

Library of Congress Catalog Card Number 2002116601
Chapman, Elwood N. and Wil McKnight
The New Supervisor, Fourth Edition
ISBN 1-56052-668-8

Learning Objectives For:

THE NEW SUPERVISOR

The objectives for *The New Supervisor, Fourth Edition* are listed below. They have been developed to guide you, the reader, to the core issues covered in this book.

THE OBJECTIVES OF THIS BOOK ARE:

❑ 1) To describe the basic responsibilities, technical skills, and attitude required to be a successful supervisor

❑ 2) To present four fundamentals every supervisor must master and to provide ideas and skills for putting them in place

❑ 3) To point out special situations that a supervisor can expect to encounter and show how to deal with them

❑ 4) To prompt you to prepare an Action Plan that incorporates the concepts and techniques from this book into your daily life

ASSESSING YOUR PROGRESS

In addition to the learning objectives, Crisp Learning has developed an **assessment** that covers the fundamental information presented in this book. A 25-item, multiple-choice and true-false questionnaire allows the reader to evaluate his or her comprehension of the subject matter. To buy the assessment and answer key, go to www.crisplearning.com and search on the book title, or call 1-800-442-7477.

Assessments should not be used in any employee selection process.

About the Authors

The late Elwood N. Chapman retired in 1977 as a professor at Chaffey College and a visiting lecturer at Claremont Graduate School after 29 years of successful college teaching. He was a graduate of the University of California. Mr. Chapman was also co-founder of Crisp Publications, and author of more than a dozen books by Crisp.

Wil McKnight, author of this fourth edition, is a writer and third-generation publisher, primarily in the areas of supervisory training, vocational education, and work study.

Mr. McKnight has a B.A. from Carnegie Mellon University (back when they called it Carnegie Tech), and an M.B.A. from Stanford. He is a co-author, with Mr. Chapman, of Crisp's *Attitude: Your Most Priceless Possession,* and has also written several self-study books and checklists for construction supervisors, some of them based on Crisp Publications. You can reach him via e-mail at wil@wilmcknight.com.

How to Use This Book

This *Fifty-Minute™ Series Book* is a unique, user-friendly product. As you read through the material, you will quickly experience the interactive nature of the book. There are numerous exercises, real-world case studies, and examples that invite your opinion, as well as checklists, tips, and concise summaries that reinforce your understanding of the concepts presented.

A Crisp Learning *Fifty-Minute™ Book* can be used in a variety of ways. Individual self-study is one of the most common. However, many organizations use *Fifty-Minute* books for pre-study before a classroom training session. Other organizations use the books as a part of a systemwide learning program—supported by video and other media based on the content in the books. Still others work with Crisp Learning to customize the material to meet their specific needs and reflect their culture. Regardless of how it is used, we hope you will join the more than 20 million satisfied learners worldwide who have completed a *Fifty-Minute Book*.

Preface

Hardly anyone ever starts from scratch. In life—personally and at work—we all build on the results of those who have gone before: family, co-workers, people who earlier shaped the environments and situations that affect us today.

This fourth edition of *The New Supervisor: Stepping Up with Confidence* builds on the foundation set by Elwood Chapman through three previous editions and his nearly 50 years of observation and reflection on such questions as: What does it take to be a successful supervisor? What should a new supervisor expect? How can new supervisors get ready for what lies ahead?

Changes in the fourth edition are subtle but important:

➤ The fourth edition contains more examples, with additional details drawn from real situations.

➤ It is more interactive: You will read; you will pause to reflect, analyze, and discuss; then you will write down ideas, conclusions, and techniques that you can *apply*.

➤ The fourth edition adds an important focus on results. Every supervisor must be productive—and must produce these results *through* other people.

➤ Finally, the structure of this book leads to *action* by prompting you to compile your response to its ideas, conclusions, and techniques into a list of *Action Ideas* that can help you improve your daily work and personal life, starting now.

An important assumption flows throughout this book: *Supervising others is both challenging and rewarding.* Supervision offers enormous potential for successful teamwork and personal growth. And you will learn and apply ideas and skills that will benefit every aspect of your life.

Wil McKnight

A Voluntary Contract

Many new supervisors find that setting success goals helps them get off to a good start. An effective way to do this is to identify, discuss, and refine such goals with your supervisor, then ask this person to monitor your progress for a 30-day period. You can use the Voluntary Contract below, which you both sign, to formalize this approach. It will help you stay focused on what is important and will show that you are sincere about your new responsibilities.

VOLUNTARY CONTRACT

I, _____ , hereby agree to meet with the person designated below within thirty (30) days to discuss the progress I have made in implementing the techniques and ideas presented in this supervisory training program.

The purpose of this meeting will be to identify and review areas where my performance has shown strength and where my performance has shown I can still improve, and to establish action steps for making those improvements.

Signed:_____

I agree to meet with the above employee on:

_____

at the following location:

_____

Signed:_____

Contents

Part 1: Meeting the Challenge

Part 2: Fitting Four Fundamentals into Your Style

Part 3: Dealing with Special Situations

Appendix

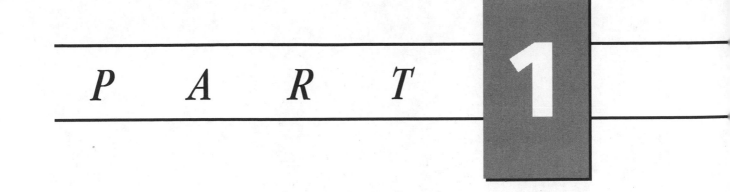

P A R T 1

Meeting the
Challenge

2

Anticipating the Challenge Ahead

Supervision is a special challenge that can help you reach new career and lifestyle goals. But becoming a successful supervisor isn't as easy as some people imagine. Three factors will require that you develop new skills and become a different kind of person on the job.

➤ The people on your staff will expect you to lead where in the past you've been their peer—and like them, a follower. This means they'll be watching your actions in the hope that you'll make quick and effective decisions and will lead them to achieve the results others expect, without cutting corners on quality or safe practices or the way you treat people.

➤ Your new role will put you in the position of being a buffer between the people you report to and those you supervise. This means you must satisfy your supervisor and, at the same time, keep your staff happy so they will maintain high standards of performance. At times this may mean it is better for you to absorb pressure from above than to pass it on to your staff.

➤ You will be *setting* standards in addition to living up to those set by others. This means you will be responsible for creating a disciplined environment where your staff understands and meets performance standards for the company or organization as well as those set by you. When variances occur, action to solve a problem-action *you* initiate—may be necessary.

The role of a supervisor isn't always easy. You'll be in the best frame of mind if you accept it as a challenge—an opportunity that will help you grow into a stronger person. An important purpose of this book is to help you *anticipate* challenges. In the space below, list three challenges you think you might have to deal with as a new supervisor.

1. _____
2. _____
3. _____

Of course, there are special rewards for those who successfully make the transition to supervisor. Some of them are listed on the next page.

What Can Success as a Supervisor Do for You?

Many things can happen to you once you become a successful supervisor, and most of them are good. Ten statements are listed below. Mark **T** if you think the statement is true or **F** if false.

As a supervisor you will:

__ 1. Increase your earnings potential

__ 2. Have opportunities to learn more and develop a new set of skills

__ 3. Gain increased respect from your family, neighbors, and friends

__ 4. Position yourself for promotion to greater responsibilities

__ 5. Have less freedom in the workplace

__ 6. Increase your self-confidence

__ 7. Increase your job satisfaction by taking responsibility for results

__ 8. Feel that you can make a difference

__ 9. Learn and develop "people skills"

__ 10. Have a greater feeling of self-worth

Check your responses against the answers shown at the bottom of the page.

Perhaps now you can think of a few more benefits from becoming a successful supervisor. If so, list them below.

1. _____

   _____

2. _____

   _____

3. _____

   _____

Anwers to the True/False Questions:

Statements 1, 2, 3, 4, 6, 7, 8, 9, and 10 are true. Statement 5 is false; supervisors normally have more freedom than the people they supervise because they have more control over their day-to-day activities.

Getting Started: Copy a Successful Supervisor

As you think about making your transition into a supervisory role, it is useful to recall successful supervisors you have known, worked for, or observed. At the start, it is often a good idea to pattern or model your behavior after a successful supervisor—someone whose effectiveness you respect.

If possible, make notes about two or three successful supervisors and the specific traits that you feel made them effective.

Who:_____

Their Responsibility:_____

Success Traits:_____

_____

Who:_____

Their Responsibility:_____

Success Traits:_____

_____

Who:_____

Their Responsibility:_____

Success Traits:_____

_____

You will discover that highly successful supervisors have much in common. If possible, discuss some of these characteristics and principles of good supervision with other supervisors—new ones like you, experienced supervisors, and the supervisor you report to.

Some common traits shared by successful supervisors—and supervisors who fail—are presented on the next page.

What Kind of Supervisor Do You Choose to Become?

Successful Supervisors. . .

➤ Are always prepared—with well-thought-out plans, clearly communicated goals, and the right resources in place

➤ Stay positive; show strength when under pressure

➤ Listen more than they talk—and work hard to become good communicators

➤ Establish high standards for quality and set a good example

➤ Take time to teach their staff what they need to know

➤ Set reasonable and consistent standards and limits

➤ Seek high productivity by building a team effort and a team spirit

➤ Ensure safe practices and a safe workplace

➤ Always seek opportunities to improve

➤ Treat everyone fairly

Add your own observations to these lists:

_____

_____

Supervisors Who Fail. . .

➤ Always react instead of thinking ahead and planning ahead

➤ Do not understand that it is not what they can do that counts—it is what *they can get others to accomplish* that is important

➤ Supervise without listening, give orders, make demands, and keep the pressure on without considering the capacity or feelings of the people who work for them

➤ Allow problems to get them down

➤ Rush in with instructions to their staff, then fail to follow up

➤ Yell and scream at staff members—and sometimes humiliate them

➤ Slack off on quality or safety when under pressure

➤ Let their status or job title go to their head and become too bossy

➤ Are more concerned with being *liked* than being *respected*

➤ Have little interest in learning about basic supervisory skills

_____

Throughout your work career, you have had many opportunities to observe common mistakes that supervisors make. In the space below, list the three most important *mistakes you plan to avoid*.

1. _____

2. _____

3. _____

Communicating Through Your Attitude

People are often promoted to supervisor because they have shown high productivity and good personal work habits. As a supervisor, your ability to obtain first-rate performance *through others* is far more important than what you can do yourself. And your attitude—as viewed by others—is critically important to obtaining excellent performance *through your staff.*

In fact, nothing will affect your relationship with the people you supervise more than your consistent—and visible—attitude. Your attitude sets the pace and the tone for everyone you work with, especially your staff. Everything you do will be reflected in the attitude of your staff. Remember, attitudes are *caught,* not taught!

Attitude is the way you look at things *mentally.* You have the power to look at your new role and new responsibilities in any way you wish. If your viewpoint is positive and enthusiastic, you'll communicate to your staff that you're *ready, willing, confident,* and able to accept your new responsibility, and they will probably meet you more than halfway. If you appear weak *in their view*—by acting uncertain, tentative, or insecure—they may interpret this to mean that your attitude is negative, and you may not receive their full support or cooperation.

On the other hand, you cannot appear power-hungry or act like a dictator. Letting your new role go to your head will give your staff a negative impression of you, causing a negative attitude in them.

As a new supervisor, many people will be watching what you do, and no matter what you may do to hide it, your attitude will show. So it's important to develop and maintain the kind of attitude that will make all your other efforts effective.

Always remember that it's your actions, not your words, that count most. Through your actions, your attitude "speaks" so loudly that it overpowers anything you say.

How Do You Feel About Becoming a Supervisor?

The exercise that follows will help you estimate your feelings and attitude about becoming a supervisor. Read each statement and circle the number that best describes how you feel now. Circle a 5 if the statement closely matches your feeling; a 2 if the statement does not describe the way you feel at all. There are no right or wrong responses to this exercise. Its purpose is to give you insight into your attitude about being a supervisor.

	< Agree		Disagree >
I take responsibility for seeing that a job is done right.	5	4	3	2
Becoming a respected supervisor is important to me.	5	4	3	2
I enjoy teamwork.	5	4	3	2
I want to understand more about human behavior.	5	4	3	2
I want to advance to positions of greater responsibility.	5	4	3	2
I want to master a wide range of supervisory skills.	5	4	3	2
I like being in a leadership role.	5	4	3	2
Working with a difficult employee would be an interesting challenge.	5	4	3	2
I want to learn how people become motivated to do first-rate work.	5	4	3	2
I'm excited about the opportunity to become a supervisor.	5	4	3	2

TOTAL _____

Author's Assessment

Add the circled numbers and write down the total. If you scored above 40, your feelings match closely with the attitude of successful supervisors. If you rated yourself between 25 and 40, you probably feel okay about being a supervisor, but you are uncertain about or need to think over some aspects of the position. A self-rating under 25 indicates that the role and responsibility of a supervisor may not be for you.

Of course, the self-assessment on the previous page is based on what you know and how you feel now. It may change—one way or the other—as you:

➤ Understand more about the responsibilities of being a supervisor.

➤ Learn basic skills and techniques that can help you become an effective supervisor.

➤ Develop a list of Action Ideas for getting started—whether it's your first day as a new supervisor or the first day of a *fresh start* in a position you've held for a while. A form for this purpose is provided in the appendix. As you read this book, note any ideas that occur to you for improving your supervisory skills. Note the page number that inspired the idea so you can return to it later to refresh your memory and polish your skills.

From time to time, it is a good idea to come back to this exercise to see how your feelings and attitude might be changing. Circle the page number.

Your Attitude About Quality

There is a direct relationship between your attitude and the quality of the work your staff turns out. When you are upbeat and focused on quality, your staff will respond in positive ways that will enhance all aspects of the work they do. If you overlook defective work, it will shape their attitude about quality in a negative way. When you are negative—expect *everything* to level off or drop.

The attitude toward quality in your company or organization will ripple out and be noticeable to customers and others—people who can affect the revenues or support you need to survive and prosper. The results of poor quality—complaints, rework, missed deadlines, budget overruns—cannot be concealed. This is true for every sector of the economy: manufacturing and service, public and private. It is true even if you are located in a distant outpost or an isolated cubicle and never see a customer face-to-face.

A negative attitude about quality at any level can eventually lead to a decrease in revenues, grants, budgets, or whatever sources provide the economic lifeline for your company, organization, department, or project.

In the space below, write the names of a few companies, organizations, departments, or projects that you feel stand out for the high quality of their work.

Name   **What They Do That Stands Out**

_____   _____

_____   _____

_____   _____

Your Attitude About Productivity

Every supervisor must have a sharp focus on results and productivity—one eye on the budget and one eye on important deadlines. But it is not enough just to keep the pressure on.

If you shortcut quality to meet production goals or lose touch with the quantity of work your staff can realistically accomplish, they may think your attitude is negative. If your only response to productivity goals is to turn up the heat, you may reflect an attitude that actually undercuts your ability to get more productivity from your staff.

On the other hand, showing up without a plan also will affect their attitude in a negative way. Technical skills—planning, organizing, focusing on results, paying attention to detail—are essential, but they are not enough. In the long run, you will get the best results by applying your technical skills with an attitude that includes *people skills* such as:

➤ Active, two-way communication

➤ Encouragement and teamwork

➤ Coaching, counseling, and training

➤ Respect for the professional talents and problem-solving skills of the people who work for you

You will learn more about applying these people skills to your supervisory role as you work your way through this book.

Your Attitude About Safety

Everyone knows that safety is a top-level concern in such industries as construction, mining, manufacturing, and healthcare. But for legal reasons and as a part of sound business practice, safety should be a vital concern for every company or organization. And safety issues have personal meaning for every supervisor.

Laws protect everyone—employees, supervisors, managers, visitors, and the general public—from unsafe working conditions. It is essential that you clearly understand your safety obligations, which, under some circumstances, may become *personal* and *legal*. Ask your supervisor to provide a copy of any safety plans or reference information that is relevant to your safety responsibilities. *You must know what is expected of you.*

And your attitude and your actions must show everyone that the work you supervise will be carried out safely, period. You must ensure that your staff is properly trained and that appropriate support resources are in place.

➤ **Proper training** covers hazards directly related to the work and the work area, materials and procedures used in carrying out the work, and general hazards that might affect anyone who comes in contact with your work location.

➤ **Appropriate support resources** include a comprehensive (written) safety program that's actually implemented, safety equipment that's always available and in proper condition for use, reference materials that are current and easily accessible to your staff, and a regular pattern of formal and informal communication with your staff about safety issues.

As with quality, everything you do about safety will be reflected in the attitude of your staff—and the attitude of your staff will affect your ability to eliminate or avoid hazards to any people involved in the work you supervise.

Reflecting on Self-Confidence

Along with a positive attitude, it takes personal self-confidence to become a successful supervisor. When you first start out, you may not have all the self-confidence you would like, *but do not lose faith in yourself.* As a supervisor, you will gradually build your personal confidence—slowly, but steadily. Remember that an increase in self-confidence is one of the benefits of becoming a supervisor in the first place.

You have the "right stuff" or at least the potential to develop the "right stuff." If you have already been selected to be a supervisor, this is an expression of the confidence others have in you. As you learn about the basic supervisory ideas, techniques, and skills covered in this book—and put them into practice—your self-confidence can grow to match the confidence others have already shown in you.

If you are not yet a supervisor, your willingness to tackle this book is an expression of self-confidence. By obtaining knowledge and preparing yourself, you'll have a solid foundation that will help you get off to a good start. And nothing builds self-confidence like a good start.

Self-confidence comes from applying your strengths and improving your weaknesses. Take a minute to reflect on your own strengths and weaknesses.

Strengths:_____

_____

How you can apply them:_____

_____

Weaknesses:_____

_____

How you can improve them:_____

_____

Rate Your Self-Confidence

This exercise will help you discover your level of self-confidence. Read each statement and circle the number that best describes how you feel about what it says.

	< Agree		Disagree >	
I am not easily intimidated when dealing with "difficult" people.	5	4	3	2
Complex technical problems do not overwhelm me.	5	4	3	2
When necessary, I can correct or discipline those who require it.	5	4	3	2
I can identify a problem, make a decision, and carry it out.	5	4	3	2
I can back up what I say, and I can back up a deserving staff member with my supervisor.	5	4	3	2
I have enough confidence to become a good teacher and coach.	5	4	3	2
I can listen, I can give good instructions, and I can explain things clearly.	5	4	3	2
I can negotiate or work out a solution among conflicting individuals' competitive interests.	5	4	3	2
I will not avoid confrontations when action must be taken.	5	4	3	2
I can say no when necessary.	5	4	3	2

TOTAL _____

Author's Assessment

Add the circled numbers and write down the total. If you scored 40 or above on this exercise and also on the attitude exercise on page 9, you have a winning combination for becoming a successful supervisor. If you scored lower on self-confidence than attitude, it is a signal that although you have the right approach to supervision, you need to develop some aspects of your basic supervisory behavior. This usually means taking one or more of the following actions: *Identifying* the specific supervisory skills you need to learn and master to become effective, *learning and mastering* the techniques and skills necessary for success, or taking a different approach or *trying a different style* in those situations where you rated yourself lower.

Taking Charge

Supervisors are *in-charge* people. As effective leaders, they use their sources of power to obtain positive results. When you assume your role as a supervisor-leader, you have three sources of power that you can tap.

First, you have *knowledge power* because of what you know. In most cases, you *know more*—have greater experience—than the individuals on your staff. When you teach them what you know or coach them in skills or techniques you have learned through experience, you make effective use of your knowledge power.

Second, you gain power from the *role* or *position* you occupy. Others will expect you to take charge. Just being the supervisor gives you authority that puts you in charge—as long as you use your authority wisely and in ways acceptable to the people you supervise.

Third, you have *personality power*. You can persuade or encourage others through your positive attitude, friendly manner, patience, persistence, and other personal characteristics.

Although you must be sensitive in the way you use your power—do not let your new position go to your head—these three sources of power can help you become the kind of supervisor you want to be. Try to think of a few ways you can use each of these sources of power as you take charge in your new responsibility.

A Note About Case Studies

The purpose of a case study is to provide insights you may not otherwise gain by just reading about ideas and skills. Five case studies are included in this book to present specific situations to think about and to show how you can *apply* important ideas and skills to real situations.

These cases do not have exact solutions or answers. Different points of view are always possible—and even encouraged—in discussions of people, their attitudes, and their behaviors. You can benefit in two ways from these case studies:

➤ By analyzing the case and expressing your views

➤ By comparing your ideas with the author's comments at the back of the book

CASE #1: WHO WILL SUCCEED?

Assume that Joe and Maria have similar experience and training. When selected to become supervisors, they adopt different attitudes toward their new role and responsibilities. Which one, in your opinion, stands the best chance of succeeding as an effective supervisor after six months? Each will supervise a staff of 10 customer service reps in a Midwest metropolitan area. It is mid-November.

Joe greeted the news of his promotion by throwing a party and inviting all his former co-workers. The next day he made a list of "dos & don'ts" he planned to follow when he took over in two weeks. Joe figured he had worked under enough supervisors—both good and bad—to know exactly what to do. He would pattern his behavior on what he had learned from observing them. Why bother to study techniques and principles in advance? Why get all uptight by too much preparation? Joe believes that personality and plain old common sense are all that are needed. His strategy will be to set a good example by personally working hard, staying close to his staff and doing a lot of listening, then concentrating on building good relationships in all directions. Joe has complete confidence in his ability to be a successful supervisor.

Maria was delighted with the announcement of her promotion. She immediately began to use the two-week period to prepare for her new responsibilities. She quickly found a couple of good books on supervision and started to make a list of recommended approaches and techniques to follow during the first few weeks. How to demonstrate authority? What planning techniques to use? What changes in behavior would be required? Maria assumed that she had a lot to learn about becoming a successful supervisor—and very little of it concerned customer service. She believes in herself, but Maria does not have Joe's level of confidence, and she decides on the following strategy: Although she intends to remain friendly and upbeat, she will slowly pull back from too much personal contact with former co-workers as a way to demonstrate her role and authority. Next she will concentrate on creating and communicating a clearly organized weekly plan so that her staff will know exactly what she expects of them.

CONTINUED

Which person, Joe or Maria, has the better chance for success? If both survive, who will probably be more effective? Will Joe, with his upbeat, confident approach do a better job than Maria with her more analytical attitude? Or will Maria, with her less confident but more deliberate strategy, outperform enthusiastic Joe? Answer these questions:

1. Will Joe still be a supervisor after six months? _____

   Why? _____

2. Will Maria still be a supervisor after six months? _____

   Why? _____

3. What are the traits that will help Joe to be an effective supervisor?

   _____

   _____

4. What are the traits that might interfere with Joe's effectiveness?

   _____

   _____

5. What are the traits that will help Maria to be an effective supervisor?

   _____

   _____

6. What are the traits that might interfere with Maria's effectiveness?

   _____

   _____

7. Assume that Joe and Maria supervise the customer service department at a retail superstore where the pace is often frenetic during the holidays. Which of these two supervisors would you rather work for?
   Why? _____

   _____

*Compare your answers with the author's suggestions
in the back of the book.*

Presenting a Strong, Effective Image

As a new supervisor, it is important for you to communicate a *take-charge* image. You must let everyone–the people who work for you, the person you report to, other supervisors, and others you work with–know that they can count on you and your staff for first-rate performance. And it must appear to be a natural transition; as a new supervisor you cannot afford to give the impression that your new position has gone to your head.

Why is a strong image necessary? First, as a supervisor, others *expect* you to be a leader. They will produce more if they know they are part of a cohesive team that knows what it must do and is prepared to focus on reaching goals and achieving first-rate performance. In contrast, a *weak* supervisor will likely cause a staff to drift–perhaps slacking off on quality, letting problems fester, or losing productivity.

How do you communicate a strong image? Consider these practices, and check (✔) those you want to include in your everyday approach.

❑ **Communicate openly and frequently with your staff.** Your staff will feel more secure and be more productive when they know you understand the work and the results you expect them to obtain, and you give them clear instructions.

❑ **Actively listen to your staff.** Listen to their ideas about the work you expect them to accomplish. Use feedback to confirm that each person has accurately received your message.

❑ **Communicate openly and frequently with your supervisors.** People will notice whether you are an effective link in the chain of communication between your supervisor and the people who work for you.

❑ **Be decisive.** Follow up communication with action. Tackle problems quickly. Take care to first identify the problem. Develop possible solutions, then be decisive when selecting and implementing the solution you choose.

❑ **Set a brisk tempo.** Move about purposefully, but not in a frenzy. Set a pace that you can maintain long-term and without strain.

❑ **Handle mistakes quickly and calmly.** When things go wrong, collect the facts, identify the problem, and develop an effective solution. Show that you can handle problems and unexpected events.

❑ **Show that you enjoy your work.** Balance your authority with a sense of humor. Help everyone have a little fun.

❑ **Check your appearance.** Do not overdo it, but look the part. Do not let your appearance become an issue to the people you report to.

❑ **Be positive.** Encourage your staff. Recognize their accomplishments. Keep in mind that your attitude and your actions affect and shape their attitude and their actions.

Getting Yourself and Your Staff Organized

If some supervisors just don't get the job done, it's often because they are poorly organized. Some are unable to organize themselves or their staff. They live and work from day to day without a plan. They arrive at the workplace, then start to figure out what the day's plan will be. They often seem to move from one crisis to another. They are "surprised" by unscheduled, but common, events such as bad weather, late deliveries, or an absent staff member. They don't have the right resources in place for the tasks at hand, they miss deadlines, and they always seem to be scrambling.

The result? Their staff feels frustrated and insecure, and they consistently fall short on performance goals, especially quality and productivity. The heat is always on, and people start to have that sinking feeling every Sunday night.

The answer? Set daily and weekly goals. Keep your primary performance goals clearly in focus by writing them down. Know what results your company or organization and your supervisor expect from you. And make sure your daily and weekly goals are aligned with these expectations. Do this by tracking your results, writing them down, and comparing them with your plans and goals so you can make adjustments as necessary. You must write things down! There is no other way. No matter how smart or motivated you are, you cannot keep track of everything in your head.

Setting Daily and Weekly Goals

Planning is simply the *thinking that comes before doing*. Planning means setting goals and objectives for your staff that support and implement the performance objectives for your department or work group. Planning enables you to put the right resources, in the right amount, in the right place, at the right time—*before* your staff starts using time and other available resources in ways that do not get results.

As a non-management employee, you could do your job without much planning. If you came to work on time, brought your skills and tools, and kept yourself in reasonably good health, you were ready to do what was expected. Normally, you then carried out tasks that your supervisor had planned or scheduled. But now you are the supervisor, and it is up to you to have a daily and weekly plan that you have reviewed and matched up with the overall plan *before* the workday or workweek begins.

The key word in these two paragraphs is *before*.

Staying Up-to-Date in Your Planning

Planning goes with the territory. If your company or organization has a planning system, use it! Revise or adjust your plan at the end of every day and every week from the work your staff actually completes. A smart supervisor will:

➤ Keep a daily "To Do" list of key tasks, listed in priority order

➤ Revise this "To Do" list at the end of each day in preparation for the next day

➤ Write daily and weekly goals in a daily planner or diary

➤ Recognize or reward staff members whenever they reach a benchmark or goal and celebrate the achievement of significant goals

➤ Keep a brief, written record of each day's work: notes on any special events or circumstances that affected quality and productivity, the number of staff on hand to do the work, the hours worked, the production achieved

Most successful supervisors operate with a daily "To Do" checklist plus a planning form that helps them look ahead. Your company or organization may have created forms or you may have obtained a commercial daily planner package. Whatever system you use should enable you to keep a clear focus on the following four areas:

➤ Key daily tasks, listed in priority order

➤ Important short-term goals (weekly or monthly) and key long-term goals (monthly or annual)

➤ Performance results:

 – Actual production vs. planned production

 – Progress vs. benchmarks and deadlines for special projects

➤ Staff development, quality initiatives, and safety activities

And remember: You must write things down!

Turning Ideas and Plans into Results

Good ideas are important and sound plans are essential. But nothing really happens until ideas and plans are turned into actions. In the appendix are two forms, one for noting *Action Ideas* and one for turning your ideas into *Action Plans*.

If you are following the Action Ideas suggestion on page 10 (in the "How Do You Feel About Becoming a Supervisor?" exercise), you have already begun developing a list of things you can *do* to improve your supervisory skills. When you have developed this list, organize your ideas into a series of Action Plans and note them on that form. An action plan is simply a list of the action ideas that would have the most potential impact on performance.

The key word is *action*. Just Do It! Then see what works and what does not. Repeat the winners and scrap the losers. Add new ideas and repeat the process—again and again and again.

Key Points from Part 1

How to Become a Successful Supervisor (p. 6)

➤ Always be prepared—with well-thought-out plans, clearly communicated goals, and the right resources in place.

➤ Stay positive; show strength when under pressure.

➤ Listen more than you talk—and work hard to become a good communicator.

➤ Establish high standards for quality and set a good example.

➤ Take time to teach your staff what they need to know.

➤ Set reasonable and consistent standards and limits.

➤ Seek high productivity by building a team effort and a team spirit.

➤ Ensure safe practices and a safe workplace.

➤ Always seek opportunities to improve.

How to Fail as a Supervisor (p. 6)

➤ Always react instead of thinking ahead or planning ahead.

➤ Focus on what you can do and rely on *your* effort, not what *you can get others to accomplish.*

➤ Supervise without listening; give orders, make demands, and keep the pressure on without considering the capacity or feelings of the people who work for you.

➤ Let problems get you down.

➤ Rush in with instructions to your staff, then fail to follow up.

➤ Yell and scream at staff members—and sometimes humiliate them.

➤ When under pressure, slack off on safety or quality.

➤ Be THE BOSS; let your status or job title go to your head.

➤ Be more concerned with being *liked* than being *respected.*

➤ Have little interest in learning about basic supervisory skills.

Communicating Through Your Attitude (p. 8)

➤ Attitude is the way you look at things *mentally.*

➤ Be positive and enthusiastic; communicate to your staff that you are *ready, willing, confident,* and *able* to accept your new responsibility.

➤ Acting uncertain, tentative, or insecure may be seen as a signal that your attitude is negative.

➤ Caution: Do not let your new role go to your head; do not shortcut quality to meet production goals; do not lose touch with the quantity of work your staff can realistically accomplish.

➤ Your attitude "speaks" so loudly that it overpowers anything you say.

Your Attitude About Quality (p. 11)

➤ Your attitude sets the pace and the tone for everyone you work with, especially your staff.

➤ If you overlook defective work, it will shape their attitude about quality in a negative way.

➤ There is a direct relationship between your attitude and the quality of the work your staff turns out.

➤ When you are upbeat and your focus is on quality, your staff will respond in positive ways; when you are negative, expect everything to drop off.

➤ The attitude toward quality in your company or organization—good or bad—will ripple out and be noticeable to customers and others who can affect the revenues or support your need to survive and prosper.

➤ The results of poor quality cannot be concealed.

Your Attitude About Productivity (p. 12)

➤ Every supervisor must have a sharp eye on results and productivity, especially budgets and important deadlines.

➤ Technical skills—planning, organizing, focus on results, attention to detail—are essential, but they are not enough.

➤ To get the best results, apply technical skills with an attitude that includes active, two-way communication; encouragement and teamwork; coaching, counseling, and training; and respect for the professional skills and problem-solving skills of the people who work for you.

Your Attitude About Safety (p. 13)

➤ Safety is a vital concern for every company or organization, and safety issues have personal meaning for every supervisor.

➤ You must clearly understand your safety obligations, which, under some circumstances, may be *personal* and *legal*.

➤ Ask your supervisor to provide a copy of any reference information or safety plans that are relevant to your safety responsibilities.

➤ You must ensure that your staff is properly trained and that appropriate support resources are in place.

➤ Everything you do about safety will be reflected in your staff's attitude and will affect your ability to eliminate or avoid safety hazards.

Reflecting on Self-Confidence (p. 14)

➤ It takes personal self-confidence to become a successful supervisor.

➤ Self-confidence comes from applying your strengths and improving your weaknesses.

➤ Your self-confidence can grow as you learn basic supervisory ideas, techniques, and skills.

Taking Charge (p. 16)

➤ Use your *knowledge power* to direct, instruct, coach, and counsel.

➤ Use the power and authority that flows from your *role* or *position* as a supervisor.

➤ Use your *personality power* and positive attitude to persuade and encourage others.

➤ Use your sources of power wisely—with care and sensitivity—and do not let your new position go to your head.

Presenting a Strong, Effective Image (p. 19)

➤ Show your ability to communicate to your staff.

➤ Show your ability to actively listen to your staff.

➤ Show your ability to communicate with your superiors.

➤ Be decisive; follow up communication with action.

➤ Set a brisk tempo.

➤ Handle mistakes quickly and calmly.

➤ Show that you enjoy your work.

➤ Check your appearance.

➤ Be a positive person.

Getting Yourself and Your Staff Organized (p. 21)

➤ Poorly organized supervisors often fail to meet expected performance targets.

➤ Set daily and weekly goals.

➤ Know what is expected of you, track your results, and compare them with your plans and goals.

➤ Write everything down.

➤ Make your plans and gather your resources before anyone starts a project or task.

Staying Up-to-Date in Your Planning (p. 22)

➤ Know exactly what results are expected of you.

➤ Be organized by having a clear, written plan—daily, weekly, monthly, and annual goals.

➤ Keep a "To Do" list of key daily tasks—listed in priority order.

➤ At the end of each day, get ready for the next day by revising your "To Do" list.

➤ Keep a brief, written record of each day's work so you can track actual performance vs. your budget and compare actual progress with important benchmarks or deadlines.

➤ Recognize people on your staff whenever they reach a benchmark or goal; celebrate significant achievements.

Turning Ideas and Plans into Results (p. 23)

➤ 1: Write down Action Ideas as you think of them.

➤ 2: Pick out the ones that have the most potential impact on performance.

➤ 3: Just Do It!

➤ 4: See what works and what does not.

➤ 5: Repeat the winners; scrap the losers.

➤ 6: Go back to Step 1.

Take a Few Minutes to Reflect

You have just finished Part 1 of this book and should have plenty of ideas and suggestions to think about. Take a few minutes to review the highlights.

➤ Go back to the Contents and look over the list of topics for Part 1.

➤ Skim through Part 1 and pay special attention to the notes and answers you have written in your book.

➤ As you go over these pages again, write any new ideas that come to mind.

➤ Use the form in the back of this book to compile a list of the most promising Action Ideas.

Think about the next few days and weeks and what is coming up at work. What opportunities and challenges stand out as you think about how you can successfully tackle what lies ahead?

Opportunities:_____

_____

_____

Challenges:_____

_____

_____

Make it a point to page through Part 1 again at some time during the next week—after you have had a chance to try out some of what you have learned. Make additional notes in your book whenever you notice something that applies to you or your staff.

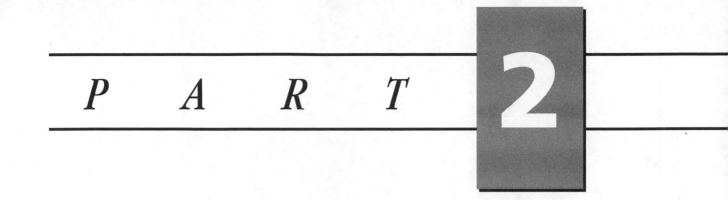

Fitting Four Fundamentals into Your Style

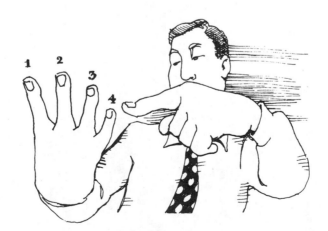

Becoming an Effective Supervisor Is Like Playing Baseball

The path toward becoming an effective supervisor can be compared to running around a baseball diamond. In baseball you must reach all four bases before you score a run that contributes to the success of your team. As a supervisor, you must master four basic principles, or fundamentals, to become effective and contribute to the success of your department or project or work group—and your company or organization.

You must constantly remind yourself that you are more like a coach or a manager than a player. Those who work *for you*—and those you *work for*—are both counting on your effectiveness and support.

You do not need to abandon the strong points that got you where you are today. But you do need to focus on the four important fundamentals that are probably new to you because they were not necessary to your earlier success.

They are *essential* now!

The Four Fundamentals of Being a Supervisor

Think of the four fundamentals of being a supervisor as the "bases" you must reach on your way toward "home."

> **First base:** Establish your authority and set reasonable standards and limits for the people you supervise.

> **Second base:** Learn how to get results *through* your staff.

> **Third base:** Become an effective coach and counselor.

> **Home:** Become a confident and respected leader.

In baseball, you win the game when you score more runs than the opposing team. As a supervisor, you win the "game" when you—*through your staff*—accomplish goals that contribute to the success of your company or organization.

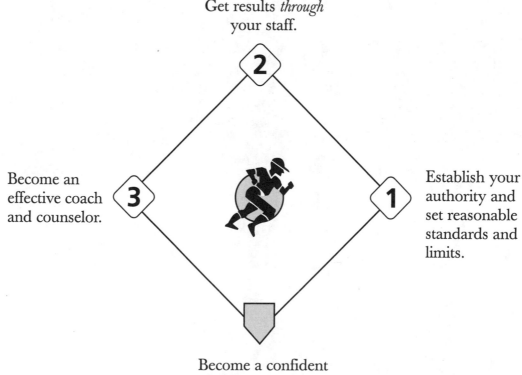

Get results *through*
your staff.

2

Become an
effective coach
and counselor.

3

Establish your
authority and
set reasonable
standards and
limits.

1

Become a confident
and respected leader.

First Base: Establishing Your Authority by Setting Reasonable Standards and Limits

To reach first base you must demonstrate you are in charge and that you know what you are doing. You achieve this by establishing your authority and setting reasonable standards and limits for the people you supervise.

Establishing and maintaining a fair, open, and healthy relationship with each staff member is a key to good supervision. To do this, you must establish your authority—not as a boss, but as the person who sets the standards and limits for your staff. These standards and limits include work performance goals and behavior standards and limits.

Everything must be well defined and clearly communicated so that each person knows what you expect—where your expectations are tight and where there is some slack. The way you communicate your standards must clearly tell each person what is expected and what is not permitted and where you will draw the line.

It is important to establish *reasonable* and *consistent* discipline. As you learn to do this, keep in mind that there is nothing inconsistent or inappropriate about showing understanding and maintaining high standards at the same time.

List below a few areas where you think it is important to set standards and limits. This is a tentative list of standards and limits you think will have the greatest impact *now*. You can always change it as you learn more about your role as a supervisor.

Standards:_____

_____

_____

_____

Limits:_____

_____

_____

_____

Making the Transition to Your Supervisory Style

You'll need to establish a style of your own—one that's both effective for accomplishing the work and comfortable for you. This may take some time and also some trial and error. As you work through the transition, give your staff some slack—and you may need to ask them to give you some slack also. You are more interested in steady, long-term results than an immediate, quick fix that will not last. This means you must establish a sound working relationship with *each person* who works for you.

In making the transition and establishing your style, consider these guidelines:

➤ Set *high*—but *attainable*—standards and reasonable limits from Day One. If you set low standards at the beginning, you will find it difficult or impossible to expect high performance later. Worse yet, if you set no standards and limits, others will drift in or rush in to set them for you. But the standards and limits they set will be *their* standards and limits, not yours; and you can bet they will not be consistent. Each person will have his or her own view, and you will have a mess!

➤ Make an effort to establish a good relationship with each staff member, on an *individual* basis, as soon as you can. Often this means listening instead of talking. It always means working to understand what makes each person "tick" and how staff members' needs can be met through the work they do. It's not a sign of weakness to seek insight or show understanding. You can be a perceptive supervisor and still be strong enough to be effective.

➤ Quickly talk with—*and listen to*—anyone who does not meet your standards or limits so they have no doubt about what you expect.

➤ Keep in mind that a few important standards and limits, *if you communicate them clearly,* are better than a long list of precise directions. Do not be a picky supervisor or someone who always tries to catch people making mistakes. Instead, set basic goals, make sure that everyone understands what to do and how to do it, then support and encourage your staff until *they are* successful. When they are successful, you will be successful also.

Most people enjoy working in an environment that has high standards and reasonable limits. In fact, they feel more secure about their jobs when their supervisor is an "in-charge" person who does not allow anyone to get by with work that is substandard or unproductive or that builds in problems for others in the company or organization.

And nothing undermines your authority faster than playing favorites. Treat each person equally—especially if some are personal friends from the days before you became a supervisor. In some situations, this may be a little difficult, but this is one challenge you must meet head-on right from the start.

Letting Go of "Business as Usual"

To remain competitive in a challenging economic environment, most companies and organizations are streamlining their operations. This often means:

➤ Expecting to meet the same or higher productivity levels and increased daily production goals—with *fewer* employees

➤ A focus on quality, continuous improvement, and challenging the "old way" of doing things

➤ Raising expectations by expecting everyone to reach a higher level of personal productivity

➤ Basing "normal" operations on tighter budgets, tighter deadlines, and a faster pace—without relaxing standards for quality or any other non-production factor

The emphasis today is on *results*. There is not much room in today's workplace for anyone who does not work smart, work hard, and build in quality.

Achieving such goals throws more responsibility on the shoulders of every supervisor. In other words, you are expected to operate in a leaner, more efficient way that will result in higher productivity—*without cutting corners anywhere*.

Some people call this running a "tight ship." This does not mean that your "crew" will be singled out or the demands on them will be excessive. And it does not mean they will become rebellious or unhappy. Just the opposite is often true because most people in the workplace like to reach goals—they enjoy performing efficiently and being part of an organization that can accomplish tough assignments on time, within a budget, and with first-rate quality.

But as the title on this page says, it probably won't be "business as usual" for you. Are you prepared, as a supervisor, to accept these higher standards and the faster tempo of productivity? The exercise on the next page will help you find out.

Can You Run a Tight Ship?

This exercise is designed to help you understand just how ready you are to run a tight ship. Answer these questions honestly—nobody is looking at this page but you.

	Yes	No	Unsure
1. Can you hold your staff to high standards without undercutting their self-motivation?	❑	❑	❑
2. Can you quickly spot and correct unacceptable behavior or work performance in a staff member without becoming upset yourself?	❑	❑	❑
3. Do you consider it a compliment when someone says you run a tight ship?	❑	❑	❑
4. Can you anticipate trouble and handle the situation before it grows into a big problem that affects quality or productivity or any other key performance factor?	❑	❑	❑
5. Can you keep your staff focused on all aspects of the work—especially quality and productivity—without being heavy-handed?	❑	❑	❑
6. Do you think it is important that your staff's record for quality is among the best?	❑	❑	❑
7. Can you meet your staff with a well-prepared work plan each day or week?	❑	❑	❑
8. Can you keep your paperwork up-to-date?	❑	❑	❑
9. Can you approach a skillful but difficult staff member in such a way that the person improves his or her behavior without becoming upset or unproductive?	❑	❑	❑
10. Can you run a tight ship without being so picky that your staff considers you a jerk instead of a good supervisor?	❑	❑	❑
TOTAL	__	__	__

Author's Assessment

Seven or more *yes* answers indicate you probably have your work under control. Seven or more *no* or *not sure* answers suggest you may have problems achieving effective and productive performance through your staff. If your total is between 3 and 7, be sure you set aside some time to reflect on the ideas presented in this book, because you are probably "on the fence" about becoming a supervisor.

Establishing Discipline

As a supervisor, you must establish discipline by setting and enforcing limits that your staff members understand. When you establish reasonable guidelines and consistently back them up, you allow people to operate with confidence because the rules are predictable—everyone knows what they are. Each supervisor must establish discipline based on the demands of the work situation and on individual style.

Think back to the *best supervisors* you have worked for—and the limits they established. List some words that describe those limits:

_____

_____

_____

_____

How did this discipline affect the results they achieved?

_____

_____

Now think back to the *worst supervisors* you have worked for and the limits they established. List some words that describe those limits:

_____

_____

_____

_____

How did this discipline affect the results they achieved?

_____

CASE #2: WHICH STRATEGY WOULD YOU USE?

Although sensitive to the capabilities and needs of her fellow workers, Angela has always set very high standards for herself. She is never late, seldom absent, and once on the job, she is all business. Angela attributes her work style to her upbringing and strict personal beliefs. She is respected by management, but she is not especially well liked by the people who work alongside her at the bank.

Yesterday Angela was promoted to teller supervisor, starting Monday. When informing her of the promotion, Angela's supervisor told her: "You were selected because we think you can put some discipline back into the teller line. It will not be easy, but we have faith in you, Angela."

Sunday night Angela sat down and developed three strategies to consider. If you were she, which strategy would you use tomorrow?

Strategy 1: Set a good example and give everyone a week or so to adjust to it.

Strategy 2: Call a staff meeting first thing and, in a low-key manner, explain the mission your supervisor has given you. Explain that the standards you will set will not only protect their jobs in the future but will give them more pride in what they are doing now. Tell them you will be firm—but reasonable and fair.

Strategy 3: Use Strategy 2 but implement it through one-on-one discussions. Call in each person and explain the changes that will be made and why.

Which strategy do you recommend that Angela employ? Why? What are its downside risks and trade-offs?

_____

_____

_____

_____

_____

*Compare your answers with the author's suggestions
in the back of the book.*

Second Base: Getting Results *Through* Your Staff

Make no mistake about it, you tackle one of supervision's toughest transitions when you realize that you cannot do it all yourself. After all, you were probably one of the better workers in the group—and it is likely that your technical skill and productivity were two of the important reasons that you were made a supervisor in the first place.

But you cannot do it all yourself. In fact, you must learn to work through—and *depend on*—others whose skills may not be quite as good as yours. Your task is to get the best result—a *team* result, not necessarily individual results—from your staff. This means you must concentrate on *four basic supervisory tasks* that are new to you and some of them have only a little to do with professional skill and productivity:

➤ Understand exactly what must be done, how it can be done, and by when it must be done

➤ Make assignments and give instructions to staff members

➤ Communicate with your staff and with the people who supervise you

➤ Follow up to see that productivity is on target and that results meet quality standards and any other important expectations

This requires a change in your viewpoint. It sounds a little tricky, but you can do it!

Earning Your Staff's Respect—and Keeping It

Now you know that intelligent supervision is more important to your success than any actual hands-on work you do yourself. Building an effective staff and developing effective relationships with the people who work for you will help you meet the challenge of getting to second base.

It is great for staff members to like you, but earning their *respect* is more important. These ideas can help you earn—and keep—the respect of the people whose performance will determine your success. As you go through the list, check (✔) those approaches that you think might be helpful to you.

❑ **Nothing builds respect better than demonstrating to your staff that you are on top of your job as a supervisor.** Show that you know what is expected, you have a clear plan for achieving those results, you can communicate that plan to your staff, and you will follow up to ensure that everything is on target.

❑ **Share your knowledge and experience.** Knowledge is also a resource, and when you share what you have learned, it can help you earn respect. Teach those who work for you everything you know that might help them become more productive, turn out better quality, and work more safely.

❑ **Create an efficient working climate, but give your staff some slack.** People make more mistakes and produce less when supervision is too close and overbearing. Your staff should be able to develop a feeling of pride in *their work*—within *your standards and limits*.

❑ **Be visible and accessible—but do not be looking over everybody's shoulder.** Give people every opportunity to do a good job and when they do, follow up with praise and compliments. When it is earned, give credit freely.

❑ **Make sure communication flows freely—in both directions—between you and your staff.** Listen to them. Encourage their suggestions and complaints. If you establish discipline that is too tight—with no slack for feedback or adjustments—you can destroy the self-motivation your staff needs to be productive and turn out quality work day after day.

❑ **Set a good example.** It may be smart to pitch in and work from time to time to remind people that your technical skills are still sharp and you have not gotten so far from the actual work that you no longer understand what you have assigned to them. But do not overdo it. Your professional skills are more valuable as a supervisor than as a producer, and remember, you will be judged by the overall performance of your staff, not by your personal productivity.

CASE #3: "THE KID"

When "The Kid" was only 22, he became an instant supervisor of a retail sales department—without any training or preparation—just before the holidays. Manny had retired in October. Margaret, who had just taken over, was abruptly transferred to another store. Leo slipped on the ice, hurt his back, and was not ready to come back to work. On Friday The Kid worked his usual shift on the floor; on Monday—ready or not—he was a supervisor.

Although he was bright and enthusiastic and did many things well, The Kid tried to do too much himself. He was a blur—scrambling around the department, hollering at the warehouse—but lines got longer and people became frustrated, even after an additional temp was added. Although there were no traumas, mistakes were made and returns ran 20% higher than expected. By mid-January, when this temporary assignment was over, The Kid was burned out and decided that being a supervisor was not for him.

But The Kid was ambitious, and he was not dumb. When his supervisor suggested that he try a couple of supervisory training courses, he signed up for a class on planning. Then he took *Leadership and Motivation*. Over the next few years, he enrolled in about 10 courses.

A few years later, The Kid had a second opportunity to become a supervisor. Realizing that he would be rated on what his department accomplished more than what he could do himself, he focused on planning the work, giving clear instructions, coaching and communicating with his staff, and making sure that the work and work flow were first-rate in every way.

Today, at 36, The Kid is no longer a kid. He is a successful store manager in a new mall—and he is still growing.

What approach should The Kid have taken 14 years ago, when he was made an instant supervisor?

_____

_____

_____

_____

*Compare your answers with the author's suggestions
in the back of the book.*

Learning How to Delegate

Supervisors who learn to delegate effectively achieve two goals at the same time. First, they gain more time to plan, organize, and maintain relationships with other employees and co-workers. Second, they help their employees become more versatile and valuable as they learn new tasks. Below are 10 typical steps in delegating. As you read through the list, think about which steps will contribute the most to your success as a supervisor and which steps you will need to work on or learn more about.

Step 1: Analyze your tasks and identify one you feel will provide you with release time—and will benefit the employee to whom you assign the responsibility.

Step 2: Consider the rotations of tasks. When done properly, rotation helps employees learn more, and boredom is less likely. And rotation may enable you to make objective comparisons of employee productivity.

Step 3: Discuss new assignments and rotation plans with the entire group to obtain feedback and generate enthusiasm.

Step 4: Select the most logical person for the task you identify and delegate it. Be careful not to overload one employee.

Step 5: Train the person you select to perform the task. Do this in appropriate detail by both explaining and demonstrating. Explain why the task is important to the total operation.

Step 6: Solicit feedback to ensure that the employee is ready to assume the new responsibility. Provide opportunities for questions.

Step 7: Allow the employee the freedom to practice the new assignment for a few days—without pressure. Over-supervision can kill motivation.

Step 8: Follow up in a positive manner. When employees have earned it, compliment them on successful performance. If improvements are required, go through the training process a second time.

Step 9: Delegate those assignments that prepare employees to take over in the absence of others—including yourself.

Step 10: Give everyone an opportunity to contribute. Solicit ideas. Use each person's special insight and ability.

Third Base: Becoming an Effective Coach and Counselor

If you are a sports fan, you know that one of a coach's primary jobs is to teach skills that help a player perform better. Supervisors are coaches who teach and encourage their "players" to improve. *Coaching* is done in the open—within the view and earshot of others.

On the other hand, some situations and problems must be handled in private—one-on-one. This is *counseling,* and the issues are more personal and sometimes touchy. When everyone works together, the team is more likely to win. Unacceptable behavior, substandard results, or personality conflicts can destroy a team. They can also destroy performance in a department, on a project, or in any work group. Every supervisor must keep a sharp eye out for any employee behavior that might undermine the group's performance. Many such problems can be solved through counseling.

More information is available in *Coaching and Counseling* by Marianne Minor, from Crisp Publications.

Viewing Yourself as a Coach

As a coach, you must plan to spend time with selected staff members so the team can win. You do this by helping them to:

➤ Learn and master a new job or skill

➤ Enhance, refine, or refresh an existing job or skill

➤ Understand the goals the team is trying to achieve—and the plans and strategies for accomplishing them

➤ Adjust to changes

➤ Handle unexpected or difficult situations

➤ Plan and implement programs and activities that enhance their career growth and advancement

If you are a sports fan, pick out a successful or championship coach—college or pro. During training camp and throughout the season, note how many ways that coach touches on the six factors listed above. You will find hundreds. You also may find that the team that wins is not necessarily the team with the most raw talent; it is the team with the best coach.

Good coaching has its rewards. When you become a first-rate coach or teacher, you will see how much more effectively you can get results *through* your staff. You will also notice some important secondary results:

➤ You will become known as someone who can develop the skills of the people who work for you—as individuals and as a coordinated team

➤ Your track record as a producer will be more noticeable to your superiors

➤ It will become easier for you to delegate

➤ You will have more time to think about and make significant decisions

➤ Your supervisor may cut you more slack

CASE #4: SYLVIA, THE COACH

Sylvia supervises a department of seven people that provides staff support to a large office. She has been a supervisor for three years, and she has received two merit increases. The department works at a brisk pace; it is productive, with staff members who have worked for Sylvia for 18 months to three years.

A new budget recently increased staffing by one; and Kevin, the new employee, was transferred from a similar department in another division. He starts Wednesday, and although Sylvia knows that things will be hectic—it is month-end and reports are due Friday—she plans to sit down with Kevin for 30 minutes first thing Wednesday morning for an orientation meeting.

Is this a wise thing for Sylvia to do on Wednesday or should she wait until after Monday's staff meeting? Why?

_____

_____

_____

When she meets with Kevin, what kinds of topics should she cover?

_____

_____

_____

Compare your answers with the author's suggestions
in the back of the book.

Using Counseling Effectively

As a supervisor, you will communicate on several levels—to individual employees, to small groups, and perhaps to large groups. Sometimes the situation will be formal and sometimes it will be informal. Whatever the situation or audience, it is clear that communication will take on new importance for you.

Communicating one-on-one with a staff member, in private, is called counseling. Once you become a supervisor, you will discover that counseling is one of your best "tools." Until you understand what counseling can do for you—and learn how to use it skillfully—it will be difficult to get to third base.

Counseling can be used to compliment good performance or to solve a problem that is hurting individual or group performance. Sometimes it is used with an employee who has violated your standards or limits and with whom you need to talk about behavior improvements. Such corrective discussions should be private, one-on-one talks. It is okay to praise in public, but it is always wise to discipline in private.

Here are 10 situations. Seven of them call for counseling; *three do not*. Check (✔) the three that are not appropriate reasons for counseling. Answers are at the bottom of the page.

❑ 1. An employee has violated your standards.

❑ 2. An employee is consistently late or absent.

❑ 3. You disagree with an employee's lifestyle.

❑ 4. An employee's productivity is down.

❑ 5. An employee behaves in such a way that the productivity of others is negatively affected.

❑ 6. You are upset.

❑ 7. Two employees have a conflict that becomes public.

❑ 8. You dislike the personality of an employee.

❑ 9. You want to compliment an employee.

❑ 10. You want to delegate a new task.

Answers to the Questions

Situations 1, 2, 4, 5, 7, 9, and 10 call for counseling by a supervisor. Situations 3, 6, and 8 do not.

When results drop off—whether it is quality or productivity or any other performance factor—you need to take action *quickly*. Problems that come up seldom solve themselves—they just fester and get worse. And as time passes, solutions that might have worked earlier become unavailable.

Of course, counseling can be a very effective way to deliver good news or recognize achievement. In fact, it is a good idea for your staff to understand that a private, one-on-one meeting does not necessarily mean that bad news is going to be delivered.

Effective counseling is not magic, it is a learned skill. Anyone can do it. And anyone can do it better with practice.

CASE #5: WILL MRT COUNSELING WORK?

Kathy learned about MRT counseling last week. The technique is based on the Mutual Reward Theory (MRT), which states that a relationship between two people can be enhanced when there is a satisfactory exchange of rewards between them.

Kathy has been having trouble with George since early last month. Today, she decided to call him into her office and discuss the situation and to see if MRT could be applied. She hopes that she can give him something he wants in exchange for a better attitude on his part.

Kathy started the counseling session by complimenting George on his consistent productivity but also telling him that she wanted him to change his behavior in three specific ways. In turn, she asked him to suggest any rewards she could provide that were within her capacity to deliver.

Kathy asked George to:

1. Continue his high productivity

2. Be more cooperative with others in the department

3. Show less hostility toward her

After thinking for a minute, George asked Kathy to provide three rewards:

1. More opportunity to learn

2. More recognition for his productivity

3. Lighter supervision—George asked Kathy to cut him some slack

George and Kathy spent 30 minutes discussing the rewards each wanted and how the other could provide them. George admitted he could be more cooperative; Kathy admitted she could provide George more opportunity to learn. And they discussed ways to accomplish this.

Will this kind of MRT counseling work for Kathy? Will it *permanently* improve the relationship between Kathy and George? Write your answer below.

_____

_____

Compare your answers with the author's suggestions
in the back of the book.

Forging Effective Relationships with Your Staff

To be an effective supervisor you need to know how to create and maintain effective relationships with the people who work for you. Good relationships are created when you:

➤ Ensure that everyone understands what is expected from your group and how those expectations fit into the goals of the company or organization

➤ Provide clear, complete instructions for all key tasks and procedures

➤ Let each person know how he or she is doing

➤ Give credit when credit is due—and if appropriate, praise in public

➤ Help each person improve through coaching and counseling that enhances strengths and diminishes weaknesses

➤ Involve people in decision-making and keep them informed on your and others' decisions that affect them

➤ Are accessible, listen, and act on the feedback others provide

The best way to *maintain* effective relationships is through frequent and open communication.

Make It Home by Becoming a Confident and Respected Leader

To be effective as a supervisor, you will want to put a strong dose of leadership into the way you work with your staff—your *style*. Everyone likes to work for a supervisor who makes it possible to stay motivated and headed in the right direction. Just as professional athletes build loyalty toward coaches who lead them to a championship, people on your staff will like to work for someone who leads them to achieve first-rate results.

Leadership means stepping out in front of others with plans that are well thought-out and with new ideas that boost results, save time, and meet expectations. You become a leader by creating *loyal staff members*—people who respect you and the results you can obtain together—perhaps even to the point where they want to continue working for you as you advance to greater responsibilities.

Becoming a supervisor is the best possible way to learn and practice leadership skills.

Leading Your Staff to New Heights

An important part of your job as a supervisor is to identify or set goals for your staff—and then lead them to achieve those goals. One important goal of *supervision* is to maintain systems and practices that are already in place.

Leadership, on the other hand, involves reaching for new heights. A leader takes prudent risks by seeking out improvements that can produce better quality and gain greater productivity. *You want to be a good supervisor, but you also want to be an effective leader.*

To become both—and to "make it home" safely—consider the following five ideas. As you read each of the paragraphs below, write down one thing you could do this week.

Be a productive supervisor. Make sure that your staff's performance is above average for your department and your organization. Watch the details. Get your reports in on time. Achieve the good feeling that comes from having everything under control.

This week:_____

Be a positive influence. Set realistic goals and help others motivate themselves to reach them. Stay positive. Sometimes it helps to keep things challenging, to keep people thinking. Do not allow anyone to become bored. Work that becomes too routine can invite carelessness toward quality, mistakes, and even accidents.

This week:_____

Help the people who work for you to reach *their* goals. Catch people doing things *right,* and praise good work whenever you see it—publicly, if appropriate. Staff members who feel good about themselves will produce better results.

This week:_____

From time to time, you may have to reestablish that you are in charge. Some staff members may need to be reminded that standards and limits exist—and they are *your* standards and limits. One way to demonstrate your authority is to handle difficult situations and to make consistent decisions.

This week:_____

Share good news. Look for positive things to talk about, especially individual achievements that affect everyone. Try to make every staff member feel that he or she is on a winning team. And do not cover up bad news. Keep it in perspective—and, if possible, try to learn something useful from every difficult situation.

This week:_____

Do You Have What It Takes to Be a Leader?

As you view yourself as a supervisor and a leader, keep in mind that most leaders develop a common set of characteristics. Check (✔) those traits from the list below that you feel you *already* possess. Effective leaders:

❑ Can communicate a sense of "being in charge"

❑ Combine individual employees into an effective team

❑ Are effective listeners

❑ Tackle tough problems as soon as these situations arise

❑ Are calculated risk takers, but not foolish gamblers

❑ Make sure staff members understand the daily, weekly, and long-term *goals* of the project

❑ Make sure staff members understand the *standards and requirements* of the project

❑ Make sure staff members understand the *realities* of the project

❑ Generate a feeling of pride in every staff member

❑ Create an active tempo in the workplace

❑ Stay cool under pressure

❑ Are energetic—in a purposeful and productive way

❑ Stand firm, but are fair

❑ Expect a high level of performance and provide an equally high level of support

❑ Back up what they say and stand up for their staff

❑ _____

❑ _____

Author's Assessment

Do not feel discouraged if you did not check too many items on this list. After all, supervision is new to you, and up to now you were not expected to have or develop these kinds of traits to be effective. So look over the list again, but this time circle the box for those traits you think you might be able to *develop*—by paying attention to them and through training—during your first year as a supervisor. Come back to this exercise every now and then during the next 12 months. Circle the page number.

Building Winning Teams

There is more to becoming a supervisor than simply a new title, a boost in the wallet, endless paperwork, and a list of meetings to attend. Every supervisor has an opportunity to mold a group of individual employees into a team.

It is true that some supervisors figure out how they can get by with a minimum amount of effort and change; they go with the flow. After all, they say, everyone generally draws from the same pool of employees, has similar equipment, and uses the same basic technology. They are satisfied with current performance or have not considered what their staff *could* accomplish with *their* leadership. Supervisors who think like this often get a rude and costly wake-up call!

Then there are others who try to turn their staff into a *team*. They seek and accept a *leadership* role. They refuse to accept the idea that their staff cannot outperform other departments on similar tasks using similar resources and technology. These leaders try to establish a special climate:

➤ There is a plan, and everybody works together to achieve it

➤ Every person in the group gives and receives communication and support to and from every other person in the group

➤ Each person tries to reach his or her potential

➤ Each staff member feels like part of a team

Setting Goals for Quality, Productivity, and Safety

Every supervisor has three key responsibilities:

1. To deliver *quality* workmanship

2. To achieve high *productivity*

3. To create and maintain a *safe* working environment

In today's competitive environment, every company or organization has goals, and these goals are usually stated in annual and monthly terms—and sometimes there are also weekly or daily expectations. There is a master plan and specific targets for various objectives and operations. There is an overall budget, which is also subdivided into a set of smaller budgets for various departments, operations, projects, and tasks. And there is a system in place to monitor actual performance and compare it to all these expectations.

In today's competitive environment, many companies and organizations have discovered that it pays to focus on *quality* with the same kind of systematic approach they have used for productivity. They set goals, design and implement programs, and keep track of results. When they follow this process through repeated cycles, they develop a system of *continuous improvement*.

Many companies and organizations also have discovered that it pays to focus on *safety* with the same kind of systematic approach they have put in place for productivity and quality. They set goals, design and implement programs, and keep track of results. Then, using their track record as a guide, they repeat the process.

So what does all this mean to you? As a leader, it is up to you to see that you and your staff begin each week and each day with a set of clearly understood goals. Some of these goals may be given to you, some of them you may have to figure out for yourself, and others you may have to ask your supervisor to provide.

List the three most important goals you are expected to accomplish through your staff.

_____

_____

_____

Helping Staff Members to Motivate Themselves

Real, sustainable motivation must come from within each person. Except for short bursts of productivity, *you* cannot significantly motivate people through pep talks (positive) or intimidation (negative). Remember the "5 & 5" rule: Most jawboning is forgotten within five minutes or five miles, whichever comes first.

But you can create and maintain a climate that encourages self-motivation. Look over the following ideas, and check (✔) those that you think are applicable to your situation:

❑ Involve staff members in some part of the goal-setting process: setting goals, communicating goals, identifying results, solving problems.

❑ Be organized—with specific goals and a plan that you clearly communicate to everyone.

❑ Make it easier for staff members to motivate themselves by creating an organized work environment where all tools, materials, supplies, and equipment needed to achieve goals are on hand and in proper working order.

❑ Be visible and accessible. Keep your finger on the pulse of the work so you know what rate of productivity is actually achieved, and understand any factors—positive or negative—that might affect quality or productivity.

❑ Do everything in your power to get rid of factors that may be demotivating to your staff. Motivation often surges when a demotivating factor is eliminated.

❑ Pass out praise and give credit—publicly, if possible—whenever someone on your staff achieves an important individual or group goal.

❑ Make a special effort to emphasize goals affecting quality as strongly as goals involving productivity, deadlines, and the budget.

❑ Promote a lively and stimulating environment through your own positive attitude. You can lead by creating and maintaining a positive work environment that enables people to motivate themselves. When you make this happen, you will find that startling results—achieved *through* your staff—will follow.

Key Points from Part 2

The Four Fundamentals of Being a Supervisor (p. 34)

➤ 1: Establish your authority by setting up reasonable standards and limits for your staff.

➤ 2: Learn how to get results *through* your staff.

➤ 3: Become an effective coach and counselor.

➤ 4: Become a confident and respected leader.

Making the Transition to Your Supervisory Style (p. 36)

➤ Set *high*—but *attainable*—standards and *reasonable* limits from Day One.

➤ Make an effort to establish a good relationship with each staff member, on an *individual* basis, as soon as you can.

➤ Quickly talk with—*and listen to*—anyone who does not meet your standards or limits so they have no doubt about what you expect.

➤ A few important standards and limits, *if you communicate them clearly,* are better than a long list of precise directions.

Letting Go of "Business as Usual" (p. 38)

➤ When you step up to supervisor, you will need to accept a new and higher performance standard and probably work at a faster tempo.

➤ You will be expected to obtain results—without cutting corners.

➤ Today's work environment often means that managers and supervisors are expected to:

- Meet the same or higher productivity levels and increased daily production goals—with *fewer* employees

- Focus on quality, continuous improvement, and challenging the "old way" of doing things

- Raise the expectations of people who work for them by expecting everyone to reach a higher level of personal productivity

- Base "normal" operations on tighter budgets, tighter deadlines, and a faster pace—without relaxing standards for quality or any other important non-production factor

➤ There is much satisfaction in being part of a company or organization that can achieve goals and in being part of a department, project, or work group that can accomplish difficult assignments.

Running a Tight Ship (p. 39)

➤ Keep control without stifling your staff's self-motivation.

➤ Quickly spot and correct unacceptable behavior or work performance in a staff member without becoming upset yourself.

➤ Consider it a compliment when someone says you run a tight ship.

➤ Anticipate trouble and handle the situation before it grows into a big problem that affects performance.

➤ Keep your staff focused on all aspects of the work—quality, productivity, and other key factors—without being heavy-handed.

➤ Make your staff's record for quality among the best.

➤ Meet your staff with a well-prepared plan each day or week.

➤ Keep your paperwork up-to-date.

➤ Approach skillful but difficult staff members in such a way that they improve their behavior without becoming upset or unproductive.

➤ Run a tight ship without being so picky that your staff considers you a jerk instead of a good supervisor.

Your Four Basic Supervisory Tasks (p. 42)

➤ Understand exactly *what* must be done, *how* it must be done, and by *when* it must be done.

➤ Make assignments and give instructions to your staff members.

➤ Communicate with your staff and with the people who supervise you.

➤ Follow up to see that the work is completed according to all relevant performance standards.

Earning Your Staff's Respect—and Keeping It (p. 43-44)

➤ Demonstrate that you are on top of your job as a supervisor.

➤ Teach those who work for you everything you know that might help them become more productive, turn out better quality, and work more safely.

➤ Create an efficient working climate, but give your staff some slack.

➤ Be visible and accessible—but do not be looking over everybody's shoulder.

➤ Give credit freely when it is earned.

➤ Make sure communication flows freely—in both directions—between you and your staff.

➤ Set a good example.

Viewing Yourself as a Coach (p. 48)

➤ Through coaching, you can deliver information and teach skills that help people who work for you to perform better.

➤ Coaching is done in the open—sometimes in groups, often one-on-one.

➤ Supervisors who become successful coaches are often highly regarded as people-developers, which can benefit them in many ways.

Using Counseling Effectively (p. 50-51)

➤ Through counseling, you improve the performance of people who work for you by affecting their behavior.

➤ Counseling is done in private–usually one-on-one.

➤ Counseling is an effective way to deliver good news and to handle problems that affect staff performance or violations of your standards or limits.

➤ Counseling is a learned skill that can be improved with practice.

Leading Your Staff Toward New Heights (p. 55)

➤ Be a productive supervisor:

– Make sure that your staff's performance is above average

– Watch the details

– Get your reports in on time

– Keep everything under control

➤ Be a positive influence.

➤ Help the people who work for you to reach *their* goals.

➤ From time to time, reestablish that you are in charge.

➤ Share good news.

What It Takes to Be a Leader (p. 56)

➤ Communicate a sense of "being in charge."

➤ Combine individual staff members into an effective team.

➤ Be an effective listener.

➤ Tackle tough problems as soon as such situations arise.

➤ Be a risk taker, but not a foolish gambler.

➤ Make staff members believe they have the *goals* of the group clearly in sight, and also the *demands* of the work and the *realities* of the work situation.

➤ Generate a feeling of pride in every staff member.

➤ Create an active tempo throughout the work area.

➤ Stay cool under pressure.

➤ Be energetic—in a purposeful and productive way.

➤ Stand firm on your principles.

➤ Expect a high level of performance; provide an equally high level of support.

Building Winning Teams (p. 57)

➤ Make sure you have a plan and that everybody is working together to achieve it.

➤ Encourage every person in the group to communicate with and support every other person in the group.

➤ Encourage and help each person achieve his or her potential.

➤ Help each staff member to feel like part of a team.

Setting Goals for Quality, Productivity, and Safety (p. 58)

➤ Make sure that your staff begins each day, week, and month with clearly understood expectations:

– The quantity of work they are expected to accomplish—how much and by when

– The level of quality they must achieve and maintain

– The requirements, resources, and actions necessary for working safely in an environment that is safe for everyone

➤ Some of these goals may be given to you, some of them you may have to figure out for yourself, and others you may have to ask your supervisor to provide.

➤ Keep track of actual performance and make adjustments as necessary.

Helping Staff Members to Motivate Themselves (p. 59)

➤ Real, sustainable motivation must come from within each person.

➤ Involve staff members in some part of the goal-setting process: setting goals, communicating goals, identifying results.

➤ Be sure that you are organized with a plan that has been clearly communicated to everyone.

➤ Create an organized work area where the resources necessary to achieve goals are available to each staff member.

➤ Pass out praise and give credit whenever a goal is achieved.

➤ Keep your finger on the pulse of the work; know what rate of productivity you have actually achieved and why.

➤ Make a special effort to emphasize goals affecting quality and other key factors as strongly as goals involving productivity and deadlines.

➤ Talk with—and listen to—all staff members regularly, especially about performance details and how they are going about their daily work to achieve results.

➤ Create a lively and stimulating environment through your own positive attitude.

Take a Few Minutes to Reflect

You have just finished Part 2 of this book—another chapter of new ideas and things to think about. This is a good time to take a break just to go over the four basic fundamentals you have been learning about.

➤ Go back to the Contents and look over the list of topics.

➤ Skim through Part 2 and pay special attention to the notes and answers you have written in your book.

➤ As you go over these pages again, write down any new ideas that come to mind. Add to your list of Action Ideas in the back of the book.

Think of the next few days and weeks and what lies ahead for you as a supervisor. What stands out in your mind as you think about how you can successfully cover each base? See if you can apply any of the Action Ideas you have accumulated so far.

1. **First base:** Establish your authority and set up reasonable standards and limits for your staff. _____

   _____

   _____

2. **Second base:** Learn how to get results through your staff. _____

   _____

   _____

3. **Third base:** Become an effective coach and counselor. _____

   _____

   _____

4. **Home:** Become a confident and respected leader. _____

   _____

   _____

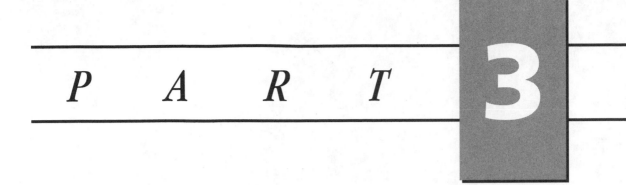

P A R T 3

Dealing with
Special Situations

Staying Positive and Overcoming the Blahs

It is not always easy to be positive. A supervisor's responsibilities sometimes feel heavy or relentless. The pressure can turn you negative, and you might not even realize it is happening. The truth is, when you are positive, your staff will notice and productivity may go up. But when you become negative, others notice that too, which also affects productivity. So your challenge is to remain positive even if the circumstances—or the people around you—are not.

Listed below are several approaches that can help you stay positive. As you read the list, assume that: (1) you are generally a positive person; (2) you can do certain things to remain positive; and (3) being aware of these activities will help you avoid that "sinking" feeling and will help pull you up when you're feeling down. Place a check (✔) by the three approaches that will help you the most.

❑ Engage in physical exercise of some kind.

❑ Pick out two or three short-term goals that are attainable, and focus on them.

❑ Make it a point to increase the time you spend with people who are positive and decrease the time you spend with people who are negative.

❑ Take a short break—a weekend or mini-vacation.

❑ Make a list of any good things that have happened at work during the last week; make another list of good things that have happened off the job.

❑ Change the way you split your time between work and leisure.

❑ Do something that improves your appearance.

❑ Help someone else achieve a goal (their goal).

❑ Talk with one or two experienced supervisors—perhaps one of the successful supervisors you listed on page 5—to learn how they deal with their occasional negativity.

List other ideas that have worked for you in the past:

_____

_____

Another Crisp book, *Attitude: Your Most Priceless Possession,* presents eight simple techniques for maintaining and recapturing a positive attitude. See the **Additional Reading** list in the back of this book for more information.

Being Alert to Troublesome Habits

Lori is an outstanding and productive paralegal, but she has a short fuse that sometimes gets her in trouble. Mark is an excellent claims rep and disaster team member, but now and then he falls into a slump that requires a lot of tolerance from everyone he works with. Chuck tries to make a pal out of everybody but becomes upset whenever co-workers do not include him in their activities.

With such characteristics, can Lori, Mark, and Chuck become successful supervisors? Yes, but only if they can break these troublesome habits. It might seem unfair, but some bad habits can be tolerated in an employee but they are unacceptable in a supervisor—the same behavior by a supervisor can spell disaster.

After holding down your job as supervisor for about three months, you will start to feel comfortable with your new role. But it is wise to take a good look in the mirror *now*, because you may need to change some habits at the beginning or they will cause you trouble every step of the way.

Read through the seven "killer" mistakes on the next page. If you tend to make any of these unforgivable mistakes, start making changes and corrections immediately or you will have difficulty as a supervisor.

Seven Unforgivable "Killer" Mistakes

You do not have to be perfect to be a successful supervisor—far from it. But some kinds of mistakes are so troublesome they can undermine everything else. Any one of these habits, if continued, will make it tough for you to succeed. If you have two or more of these shortcomings—and cannot get rid of them—you are likely to fail.

1. **Treating individuals unequally because of age, sex, culture, personal or educational background, and so on.** Sometimes this shows up as favoritism toward—or bias against—selected individuals or groups. Sometimes such treatment is open and sometimes it is subtle. Either way, it is a killer.

2. **Breaking trust with a co-worker.** The fastest way to destroy a relationship is to make a promise, then fail to keep it.

3. **Blowing hot and cold.** Consistent behavior is essential when supervising others. If you act like a drill sergeant on Monday and a slacker on Thursday, your staff will not know how to react to these mixed messages, and it will be hard to hold their respect.

4. **Failing to follow basic company policies and procedures.** Every company has certain policies and procedures that are "hard rules." Usually these rules are written down, but not always, and it is your job to know exactly what they are. If you cut corners or break these rules, you are asking for trouble. Be especially watchful for rules that relate to quality and safety, because they sometime get less emphasis than productivity rules—until something bad happens!

5. **Losing your cool in front of others.** Everyone reaches a breaking point now and then; but as a supervisor, you need to keep your temper in check. Blowing up can destroy relationships, and it is seldom an effective way to increase productivity or win your point.

6. **Having a personal relationship with someone you supervise.** You cannot do it. You simply have to choose between being a supervisor and having a personal relationship with someone you supervise. If you try to keep this candle lit at both ends, one or both of you will get burned.

7. **Failing to focus on results.** You must clearly understand what is expected of you, even if it is not written down or explained to you. You must know what productivity you and your staff are expected to produce; what quality standards your work is to meet; and what safety rules and procedures to follow. You cannot be naïve or turn a blind eye to expected results in any of these areas.

If you feel that any of these habits is something you need to correct, circle this page number or bend back the corner, and make a note on your calendar to follow up every week or so. These really are "killer" mistakes, and if any of them are troublesome to you, you simply cannot afford to ignore them.

Supervising People Who Used to Be Peers

On Friday, you and Chris worked side-by-side as peers. You were both skilled professionals, you had similar work assignments, similar titles, and similar status. You worked *with* Chris and several others, and it was a productive, first-rate team.

But on Monday, you will become the team supervisor; Chris and the others will work *for* you. This can be a touchy transition because so many things will change—job assignments, job titles, and status inside and outside the workplace.

So assume it is Sunday evening, and you are thinking about Monday morning—your first day as supervisor. Here are a few things to keep in mind as you think through this touchy transition:

➤ Stay warm and friendly, but slowly put a little distance between you and your former peers. You cannot be a pal anymore—at least in the same way you used to be a pal—and be a supervisor at the same time.

➤ Do not let someone who used to work side-by-side with you gain special treatment. If you play favorites, you will be in trouble. And once you start playing favorites, it is almost impossible to stop.

➤ Do not act as if your promotion makes you the expert on everything. Your brain was not invaded by the Master of All Knowledge over the weekend—and your staff knows it. In fact, there will probably be specific cases in which someone on your staff knows about a good solution that you do not. True, it is your responsibility to see that problems are solved, but you will be in a stronger position to get results *through* your staff if you develop the people who work for you into a problem-solving resource.

➤ Do what you can to make everyone's job a little better than it was before you became supervisor. Pay special attention to any mistakes that you used to grumble about. You do not want people to feel that you thought something was out of whack before but everybody should put up with it now that you are the supervisor.

➤ Help your staff members improve their knowledge and skills any way you can. Coach them. Find out about any training opportunities that your company or organization makes available, and make sure that the staff knows about them.

➤ Give everyone recognition for good work—especially staff members who used to work side-by-side with you.

➤ The supervisor you work for probably went through the same transition you are working through now. Ask for feedback on how you are doing and listen carefully.

If you can, think back to the last two times you got a new supervisor. If those people did specific things that eased the transition, list them below. If they made any major mistakes, note those also.

Good things:_____

_____

_____

Mistakes:_____

_____

_____

Handling Possible Resentment

Maybe not everyone is 100% thrilled that *you* were the one selected to become supervisor. Maybe there was competition and the first runner-up will be working for *you*. Maybe someone thinks that he or she (or another person) is more qualified than you are. Feelings of resentment, if they exist, might be obvious or they might be subtle. You do not want to look for problems where none exist, but it is wise to consider all the possibilities and how you could handle any reactions that might be troublesome.

If you sense the possibility of resentment over your promotion, keep these ideas in mind:

➤ The job is no longer up for grabs; it is yours. *Be the supervisor* from Day One. Do not hang back just because someone disagrees—or because you think someone might disagree—with your promotion.

➤ Direct everyone's *focus on the work* and the results that your staff is expected to accomplish. Focus on getting results *through* your staff. Look for opportunities to recognize and encourage every accomplishment, especially team accomplishments.

➤ Double your efforts to *listen;* be *visible* and *accessible*.

➤ Being a supervisor is not a popularity contest. It is more important to be *respected* than to be liked. If the respect you earn is based on results you obtain *through* your staff, then it will generate respect and recognition for them also.

➤ Talk about the situation with your supervisor; ask for advice.

➤ If you encounter obvious resentment from a staff member and it begins to affect the group's performance, you may need to use the counseling techniques suggested for handling a problem employee and dealing with conflict among staff members.

Developing Your People Skills

As an employee, your productivity was probably a *personal* measure—how much did *you* produce? Perhaps an accounting system collected data about your personal productivity or maybe your results were not tracked, but you were expected to handle a production task in an efficient, professional manner. Either way, it is likely that your personal productivity—which was probably above average—was a factor in your promotion to supervisor.

As a supervisor, however, you are now measured by your staff's productivity, and your performance depends on how well *they* perform. If the way you employ people skills enables your staff to be productive, you will do a good job. If productivity drops or quality falls off, your job may be in jeopardy. You are not a producer any more; your first priority is to get productivity from other producers.

True or False?

To check your progress and your understanding of these ideas, answer the following true or false questions. The answers are at the bottom of the page.

__ 1. Helping staff members reach their productivity potential is a high priority for a supervisor.

__ 2. Dealing with a drop in productivity by a reliable staff member should be deferred because it might cause resentment.

__ 3. A work group will often produce more for one supervisor than for another.

__ 4. A disruptive staff member who reduces others' productivity must be dealt with immediately.

__ 5. Staff members with average personal productivity can boost the productivity of others so much that they are still highly regarded.

__ 6. Most employees have higher productivity potential than they realize.

__ 7. Generally speaking, people feel better about themselves when they are more productive.

__ 8. People skills are easier to learn than technical skills.

__ 9. A skillful supervisor can have a highly productive staff without personally becoming a producer.

__ 10. A "golden" staff member is one who produces at a high level and also contributes measurably to the productivity of co-workers.

Answers to the True/False Questions

Statements 1, 3, 4, 5, 6, 7, 9, and 10 are true. Statements 2 and 8 are false. It is important to deal quickly and decisively with any drop in productivity; star producers are not exempt. People skills are usually more difficult to master.

Solving Problems

Every supervisor encounters events and circumstances that require effective problem solving. Your ability to solve problems will have a significant impact on your success as a supervisor. Problem solving is a skill, and like most skills, it can be learned and you can expect to improve your skill with practice and experience.

Problem solving is part of your everyday life, and some days it will seem like the problems are coming at you from several directions all at once. You will find it helpful to sort problems into the following four categories:

➤ **Minor people-centered problems:** requests that you can handle quickly according to acceptable practices. Occasionally you might make an exception to the standard rules, especially if your staff's overall performance is not likely to suffer and the exception does not affect others with whom you work.

➤ **Major people-centered problems:** a hostile employee, a person whose skills are not up to the job's requirements, coordination difficulties with other departments and work groups. Much time may be required to solve major people-centered problems.

➤ **Minor job-centered problems:** adjustments that need to be made to short-term plans, work procedures, resources on hand. Minimum time and effort is required.

➤ **Major job-centered problems:** special problems that require time, resources, a systematic procedure, and maybe other supervisors.

To solve problems, keep a cool head and follow this eight-step procedure:

1. Identify the *real* problem, which may be concealed by various symptoms of the problem. The real problem is the one factor that, if changed or eliminated, would cause all the symptoms to fade or disappear. Merely fixing a symptom will not do that.

2. Gather data and information about the problem.

3. Analyze the data and information.

4. Discuss your observations and conclusions with others.

5. Identify possible solutions and their costs and benefits.

6. Make a decision by choosing one of the possible solutions.

7. Implement—and communicate—the solution.

8. Follow up to see if the solution actually solved the problem. If not, start again at the top.

Effective supervisors often keep a problem-solving list, each day adding new items and crossing off problems they have solved. Some supervisors find it useful to keep a notebook. Some problems are repeaters; and a written history of symptoms, data, analyses, solutions, and results can be a valuable resource.

It is usually wise to keep your own supervisor informed about major problems you are working on. He or she may also be a good problem-solving resource.

Identifying the Problem Employee

Every supervisor must occasionally deal with a difficult staff member. Nobody is perfect, and you are smart to allow enough slack that your staff does not feel that you are always looking over everybody's shoulder. But from time to time you will have a staff member who repeatedly causes problems or difficulties.

Some people seem unable to work effectively with their peers. Others fail to follow established rules and procedures or make mistakes that cause rework or customer complaints. Still others are consistently late or absent from work. You might encounter a person who repeatedly challenges your position or tries to get under your skin. In extreme cases, a problem employee may carry hostility toward another employee, toward you, or toward someone else in the workplace.

How you deal with difficult staff members and convert them into team players is a critical part of your job. The suggestions on the next page will help you get started on the right foot when you encounter this special situation.

Special Note: This discussion assumes that you want to keep this employee and help the person become a productive staff member. Of course, another obvious solution is to replace the problem employee—fire her or lay him off. If you choose one of these solutions, *notify your own supervisor first* and be absolutely certain that you know and follow your company or organization's procedures for disciplining or terminating an employee. If you do not handle this properly, you just might exchange your problem employee for another set of problems called *wrongful termination*. It is a lousy trade.

For more information on proper procedures for terminating employees, read *Rightful Termination* by Ron Visconti, Crisp Publications.

Dealing with a Problem Employee

Here are 10 possible ways you could react to a staff member who is demanding, hostile, and disruptive. Some are effective; some are not and might even make the situation worse.

Assume that your problem employee (PE) has just blown up again. Many possible approaches are listed below. Read through the list and think about how you might handle your PE's blowup. Remember, we are talking about your *initial, on-the-spot* reaction, not an action that you might take later. It is just the beginning, but your ability to handle a tough situation successfully is much improved if you get off to an effective start. Make a thoughtful choice before you react.

➤ Stay cool. Let PE express anger without an immediate reaction from you.

Yes. *You want to solve the problem, not win an argument. Listening may help you understand the cause of PE's behavior.*

➤ Let PE know that you consider him or her to be a problem.

No. *It is not PE, the person, that is the problem, it is what PE does (or does not do). You want to change PE's behavior, not PE the person (or else this discussion would be about termination).*

➤ Challenge PE with a tough look and a firm response.

No. *There is little to be gained by backing PE into a corner—and there may be a lot to lose.*

➤ Consider PE's behavior as objectively as possible and refuse to take things personally.

Yes. *This is a productivity matter, not a personal contest. You want to reestablish PE as a contributing and productive member of your team.*

➤ Avoid the problem. Time will solve it.

No. *Problems that are ignored usually do not go away—and they often get worse.*

➤ Tell PE to hold it while you go get your supervisor.

   No. *PE is your staff member and this is your problem to solve. If this same scenario happens repeatedly, however, then it is probably appropriate to involve someone else.*

➤ Tell PE that you are just going to listen and write down the points he or she is making, then you will discuss the matter later when he or she is calmer.

   Yes. *But be sure you explain why you are writing notes or PE might feel threatened by your note taking. And do not let the pause become a delay.*

➤ Challenge PE to stop giving you a problem.

   No. *This is not a one-time occurrence to be squelched by a challenge; it is a recurring problem that needs to be figured out and solved.*

➤ Get angry and give back the kind of behavior you receive.

   No. *Your goal is to solve a problem, not win a confrontation.*

➤ In a calm manner, say, "Let's go over to my office and talk about this."

   Yes—*or go to some other location that provides enough privacy that you can have a one-on-one discussion.*

The best way to maintain your standards and limits in a situation like this is to be firm, to listen, and to be reasonable and fair.

Handling Conflict Among Staff Members

Sometimes a conflict will arise among your staff members that does not directly involve you, but you predict that it will affect group performance. The performance goals your staff needs to meet may be at risk. Because one of the four basic fundamentals of supervision is to *get results through your staff,* this kind of conflict becomes your problem to solve, and you must step in and handle it. Here is a six-point approach for handling this kind of conflict.

1. **Identify the people** who have a real stake in the matter. Separate the by-standers, supporters, and others who are naturally curious about what is going on. It is often difficult to sort out a touchy situation, and audience participation usually does not help. Move to a location where you have privacy.

2. **Listen** to each person's viewpoint. If it is a complicated situation or if you expect it to drag on for a while, take notes so you do not have to rely on your memory (or someone else's) to recall what was said. Throughout, take care to preserve the self-respect of everyone involved, and try to put yourself in each person's shoes. If you can, end the interview on a positive note.

3. **Figure out the source** of the conflict. It is often in one of these four areas:

   - People have different goals

   - There is no disagreement about the goal, but people are using ineffective or incompatible methods to reach the goal

   - People do not have the same information or they interpret information much differently

   - People have angry or negative feelings toward each other

4. **Figure out a solution** that passes this test: *This solution will enable me to get consistent, acceptable results through my staff.*

5. **Implement the solution** by negotiating acceptance from the persons directly involved in the conflict.

6. **Follow up:** Did the solution work? Did the solution stay in place? If the answer to either question is *no,* go back to the top of this six-point list and go through each step again until the answer to both questions is *yes.*

Special Note: The ideas presented on this page apply to verbal conflicts only. Make sure everyone understands that if the conflict becomes physical, you will immediately notify your supervisor and start your company or organization's standard disciplinary process for all participants.

Working with Other Departments and Work Groups

Every activity in business is connected to—and depends on—other activities. Supervisors deal with a wide range of people—within and outside the company or organization. Your staff is connected to other departments and work groups; to people who perform tasks that precede you, follow you, or work side-by-side; to vendors and suppliers; and to others who are involved in your work flow from time to time. As a supervisor, you will work with other supervisors daily. Here are some suggestions to make those important working relationships successful:

➤ **Develop a "big picture"** view that goes beyond the scope of the work your staff performs. Understand as much as you can about the overall process and your role in it—and how the results you obtain through your staff fit in the overall plan. Be aware of any special factors or circumstances that can significantly affect your staff and others.

➤ **Plan your work thoroughly.** If it might help you meet your performance goals, make your plans available to others. As the work flows, keep your head up and eyes open to notice any changes or developments elsewhere that might affect your plan.

➤ **Listen and communicate**—to your staff, to other supervisors, to your supervisor, to outsiders you work with. Think of yourself as a member of a team of supervisors—with your own supervisor as the "supervisor" of that "team." Then do your best to make this team as effective as you expect your staff to be.

➤ Without making a big noise or putting on a show, **make your standards and limits known.** It is important for other supervisors and work groups to understand the key guidelines that determine the way your staff works together to get results. And it is just as important for you to understand the standards, limits, and guidelines by which other supervisors and their work groups operate.

➤ **Use other supervisors as a resource**—for solving problems; for ideas on better ways to do the work; for information that might affect your plans. And support other supervisors with solutions, ideas, and useful information.

Do your best to make your staff the kind of first-rate staff that every other supervisor, department, and "team" really wants to work with.

Keeping Your Supervisor Happy

When you become a supervisor, it is important to keep your staff productive, meeting its performance targets and turning out first-rate quality. It is also important to make sure that you meet the expectations of the people who supervise you. In many ways, you are caught in the middle, a "buffer" who must be concerned with perceptions and relationships in both directions.

Here are four suggestions to help you develop and maintain a healthy, open relationship with the person you work directly for:

➤ Make sure that every goal you set is consistent with the goals of the company or organization or business unit you are part of. This means listening to changes that come out of meetings with your peers and your supervisor or are sent from the home office, then adjusting the goals you have set for your staff. You do not—and you cannot—work in isolation. The Lone Ranger is a fictional hero, and it is unlikely that you included him among the successful supervisors you listed on page 5.

➤ Keep your supervisor informed. *Share all the news*—the good, the bad, and the ugly. When there is any significant news about your staff or their performance, make sure you are the one who delivers that news, even if it is information you wish you did not have to report. Especially if it is bad news, resist the temptation to delay.

➤ Think ahead and plan ahead. By thinking and planning ahead, you can eliminate or avoid many surprises. And you can often *reduce the effect* of surprises you cannot eliminate or avoid. Make sure you do not ambush your supervisor with surprises!

➤ Just as your staff members are on a team, you are also on a team consisting of other supervisors like yourself. Be an effective team member. In today's work environment, things move at a brisk pace and are very interdependent. You must keep your head up and stay aware of the overall progress of adjacent work groups, upstream organizational units, and your company or organization. Support other supervisors with clear communication, solutions, and resources in the same way you want the people who work for you to support each other.

Remember that it is your responsibility to get results *through* your staff. Likewise, it is your supervisor's responsibility to get results *through you* and other supervisors like you. Make sure you are one of the people who makes those results happen.

And do not forget that your supervisor is probably trying to implement the same fundamentals that you are. Take a minute—turn back to page 34—and mentally "round the bases" from your supervisor's point of view.

CASE #6: BETWEEN A ROCK AND A HARD PLACE

Charlie, a carpenter foreman with a crew of four, was sent by Fred, his superintendent, to an OSHA seminar Friday afternoon. About 3:45, Fred noticed Charlie's crew gathered together under a tree at the edge of the job site, talking and joking with each other. First thing Monday, Fred reprimanded Charlie about his goof-off crew. Charlie, annoyed at what Fred had seen in his absence, replied, "This will not ever happen again," and promised to handle it. At their daily briefing, Charlie chewed out his crew. But then one of them explained: They'd finished out a very productive week—a total of 3,400 square feet of forms for the retaining wall foundation—by putting 750 square feet in place on Friday. It was too late to start another section, so they knocked off a few minutes early and had a spontaneous celebration of the week's accomplishment. Fred, while walking by, had seen and misinterpreted their behavior.

How should Charlie handle this situation?

_____

_____

_____

_____

_____

Compare your answers with the author's suggestions
in the back of the book.

For more information on working effectively with your supervisor, read *Customer Satisfaction: Practical Tools for Building Important Relationships* by Dru Scott, Crisp Publications.

Resolving Mistakes

Everyone makes mistakes—in fact, someone who attempts to avoid all mistakes is probably too timid and cautious to be an effective supervisor. It is how you resolve mistakes that counts.

Technical Mistakes

Supervisors make technical or mechanical mistakes when they fail to plan ahead, give faulty instructions, order the wrong materials, and so on. These mistakes are often corrected by applying extra hours and using resources that were not in the budget. The fix is usually not complicated, but it may be costly—in dollars and in time.

Mistakes Involving People

As a new supervisor, you will make your share of mistakes that affect people you work with. Again, it is how you handle these "people mistakes" that counts.

Lesson 1: *Do not be surprised* when you make a mistake that affects a relationship with someone you work with.

Lesson 2 is more important: When you make a "people mistake," *repair the working relationship immediately.* If you allow these mistakes to go unattended, you will undercut your ability to get results *through* other people. This can happen if a staff member becomes angry and cuts back on productivity or starts grumbling to others. Injuring your staff's performance is the last thing you would ever intentionally do, but if you do not handle people mistakes quickly, it will happen.

There is not one "right way" to handle a people mistake, but you will probably find these four approaches helpful.

➤ Above all, be honest about the mistake you have made. There are *reasons* and there are *excuses,* and the people who work for you are smart enough to know the difference.

➤ Acknowledge that you made a mistake. It is sometimes difficult to admit a mistake, but that is often the first step in correcting it. Apologize in an appropriate way, and show that you do not intend to make this mistake again. If some further action is necessary to "set things right," take that action as soon as you can so the matter does not fester.

➤ Talk one-on-one with the other person(s) involved so they can get anything bothering them out in the open. Communication is the best way to restore an effective working relationship.

➤ Make a reminder note to yourself about what you did that caused the problem so you are less likely to repeat this mistake. It is okay to make mistakes; it is not okay to repeat them.

For more information on correcting and avoiding "people" mistakes, read *Winning at Human Relations* by Elwood N. Chapman and Barb Wingfield, Crisp Publications.

Getting a First-Rate Staff and Keeping It

As a supervisor, you may or may not be personally involved in selecting or assembling your staff. Some supervisors have a lot of control over staff assignments and selection; some must accomplish the work through personnel they have inherited. Sometimes staff members can affect their assignments by requesting to work on a specific project or with a specific supervisor.

No matter which of these factors is in effect, one fact is clear: You want to get and keep the very best staff you can. After all, your success depends on getting results *through* your staff. You do not want defective tools, you do not want poorly maintained equipment, and you do not want your performance to depend on a second-rate staff. In each case—tools, equipment, and people—you might encounter limits to the quality of the resources you have to work with, but it is smart to put yourself in position to get the very best available.

Your best strategy is to make yourself the kind of supervisor that first-rate professionals *want* to work for—a supervisor that skillful, dependable people will *ask* to work for if they have the chance to do so. You are a new supervisor now, so this must be a long-term strategy. So think ahead five years; the following are the kinds of comments you *want* people to be saying behind your back:

➤ *"Two years, merit increases all around—amazing!"*

➤ *"Her staff really turns out first-rate work; there's hardly ever any mistakes."*

➤ *"His department always seems to come through—on time and under budget."*

➤ *"They always seem to give her the really tough and interesting projects."*

➤ *"That company has a lot of repeat clients, and you know, on the last project, the client asked for her to be in charge."*

➤ *"I hear he's tough, but his people really put out the work."*

➤ *"I'd like to work in that department, but it is only a five-person staff and three of them have been together for over two years now."*

The same strategy will work for *keeping* a first-rate staff. You want your staff members to be saying the same kinds of things:

➤　*"We* did it again—hit our target every quarter, and everybody got a merit."

➤　*"We* really turn out first-rate work; there's hardly ever any mistakes."

➤　*"Our team* always seems to come through—on time and under budget."

➤　"They always seem to give *us* the really tough and interesting jobs."

In addition to getting and keeping a first-rate staff, you want your staff members to continuously *improve* and *upgrade* their skills and work procedures. For them, this is accomplished the same way it is for you—through systematic training. Help them find it.

For more ideas, read *Retaining Your Employees* by Janice Berry and Barb Wingfield, Crisp Publications.

Pulling Together

An outstanding coach is someone who designs and implements strategies that enable the team to win. Effective supervisors can also develop winning strategies. They devise plans that keep performance at a consistent, high level. To make the plan work, each team member must perform at or near his or her potential—and team members must support each other. When everyone contributes, everyone wins.

Winning coaches (and supervisors) help their players to motivate themselves—to live up to their personal expectations and take pride in the team's achievements. They do this by:

➤ Maintaining a sense of purpose, keeping everyone focused on the performance results the team wants to achieve

➤ Communicating and encouraging everyone's involvement in the "game plan" for the day, the week, the month

➤ Seeking a commitment to first-rate performance from each staff member

➤ Making it easier for staff members to motivate themselves by creating an organized work space where all resources needed to achieve goals are on hand and available

➤ Moving quickly and assertively to remove any factor that is de-motivating

➤ Ensuring that team members take good care of themselves and avoid injury or burnout

➤ Helping staff members to improve their individual skills and to develop their role within the team

➤ Providing support and encouragement for each team member, even when short-term individual performance is not up to expectations

➤ Seeing that the *team* is rewarded as a group, even if special recognition is given to one or two people for unusually good individual performance

People who become effective, first-rate supervisors also become candidates for promotion to greater responsibilities. In supervision, it is extremely important to get started on the right foot. If you weave the ideas, strategies, and skills you have learned in this book into your everyday work pattern, you will become prepared for greater and more challenging responsibilities.

A final caution: Do not make the mistake of saying to yourself that effective supervision is simply common sense or that supervisory training is a one-time vaccination. It is much more than that. You must regularly review the skills you have learned and expand your range, paying attention to your mistakes and also learning from them.

Make your goal *continuous improvement* and the best way to accomplish this is to have a vigorous Action Plan that you continuously refresh with new Action Ideas.

Looking Ahead: Continuing Your Supervisory Training

You have learned a lot from this book, but you do not yet know it all! Think of what you have learned so far as your first step. And think of it as a strategy to get you off on the right foot—running at a pace and moving in a direction that will help you to be successful.

One thing is certain: What you have learned so far is a solid foundation on which you can build:

➤ By taking advantage of any opportunity to learn about—in greater depth—the kinds of topics you have studied in this book

➤ By combining what you have learned with your day-to-day experience on the job.

As you look ahead to your future as a supervisor, keep these ideas in the back of your mind:

➤ Nothing beats the positive effect of a good start. This applies to your first few weeks as a supervisor—and it also continues to apply to the way you:

  – Start a new project

  – Start working with a new staff member

  – Start each new day—especially Monday!

➤ The more you apply the basic principles and simple techniques you have learned in this book, the better your start will be.

➤ If you keep this book handy and review it from time to time during the next few months, you will be more likely to stay focused on what is important and to remember the basic ideas, principles, and techniques you have just learned.

➤ Once you can handle the basics, you will gradually become more confident and able to handle more difficult situations and problems. You will be able to spot more opportunities and take advantage of them.

Take a close look at the Additional Reading list in the back of this book. It will give you lots of ideas and resources for continuing your supervisory training.

Key Points from Part 3

Overcoming Your Own Periodic Negativity (p. 69)

➤ Engage in physical exercise.

➤ Pick out two or three goals that are attainable and focus on them.

➤ Increase the time you spend with positive people and decrease the time you spend with people who are generally negative.

➤ Take a short break—a weekend or mini-vacation.

➤ Make a list of any good things that happened at work last week; make another list of good things that happened off the job.

➤ Change the way you split your time between work and leisure.

➤ Do something that improves your appearance.

➤ Help someone else achieve a goal (their goal).

➤ Talk with one or two experienced supervisors to learn how they overcome occasional negativity.

Seven Unforgivable "Killer" Mistakes (p. 71-72)

➤ Treating individuals unequally.

➤ Breaking trust with a co-worker.

➤ Blowing hot and cold.

➤ Failing to follow basic company policies and procedures.

➤ Losing your cool in front of others.

➤ Having a personal relationship with someone you supervise.

➤ Failing to focus on results.

Supervising People Who Used to Be Peers (p. 73-74)

➤ Stay warm and friendly, but slowly put a little distance between yourself and your former peers.

➤ Do not let a staff member who used to work side-by-side with you gain special treatment.

➤ Do not act as if your promotion makes you the expert on everything.

➤ Do what you can to make everyone's job a little better than it was before you became the supervisor.

➤ Help staff members improve their knowledge and skills.

➤ Give everyone recognition for good work—especially people who used to work side-by-side with you.

➤ Ask your supervisor for feedback on how you are doing, and listen carefully.

Handling Possible Resentment (p. 75)

➤ The job is yours. *Be the supervisor* from Day One.

➤ Direct everyone's *focus on the work* and the results that your staff is expected to accomplish.

➤ Look for opportunities to recognize and encourage every accomplishment, especially team accomplishments.

➤ Double your efforts to *listen;* be *visible* and *accessible*.

➤ Being a supervisor is not a popularity contest. It is more important to be *respected* than to be liked.

➤ Talk about the situation with your supervisor; ask for advice.

➤ Use counseling techniques to handle difficult situations.

Developing Your People Skills (p. 76-77)

➤ Help each staff member reach his or her productivity potential.

➤ Deal immediately with a drop in productivity by a reliable staff member.

➤ Deal immediately with a disruptive staff member whose behavior reduces others' productivity.

➤ Staff members with average personal productivity can boost the productivity of others so much that they are still highly regarded.

➤ A "golden" staff member is one who produces at a high level and also contributes measurably to the productivity of co-workers.

➤ Most employees have higher productivity potential than they realize.

➤ People usually feel better about themselves when they are more productive.

➤ People skills are more difficult to learn than technical skills.

➤ A skillful supervisor must develop a highly productive staff without personally becoming a producer.

➤ A work group will often produce more for one supervisor than for another.

Solving Problems (p. 78-79)

➤ Identify the real problem, which may be concealed by various symptoms of the problem. Remember: The real problem is the one factor that, if changed or eliminated, would cause all the symptoms to fade or disappear.

➤ Gather data and information about the problem.

➤ Analyze the data and information.

➤ Discuss your observations and conclusions with others.

➤ Identify possible solutions and their costs and benefits.

➤ Make a decision by choosing one of the possible solutions.

➤ Implement—and communicate—the solution.

➤ Follow up to see if the solution solved the problem. If it didn't, start again at the top.

Dealing with a Problem Employee (p. 81-82)

➤ Stay cool; do not get angry or give back the kind of behavior you receive.

➤ Remember, it is not PE *the person* that is the problem, it is what the PE *does* (or does not do). Change the *behavior,* not the person.

➤ Do not back the PE into a corner or try to squelch the person's behavior by challenging him or her to stop giving you a problem.

➤ Consider the PE's behavior as objectively as possible and refuse to take things personally.

➤ Do not avoid the problem and do not avoid the PE; take the initiative, be interested, listen and communicate, and address the situation ASAP.

➤ Do not try to pass the problem off to someone else; this is your staff member and it is your problem to solve.

➤ To talk, go to your office or some other location that is private.

Handling Conflict Among Staff Members (p. 83)

➤ Identify the people who have a real stake in the matter; sort out the bystanders, supporters, and others who are just curious.

➤ Listen to each person's viewpoint and take notes so you do not have to rely on your memory (or someone else's) to recall what was said.

➤ Figure out the source of the conflict: different goals; ineffective or incompatible methods to reach a goal; different information or different interpretations of information; angry or negative feelings.

➤ Figure out a solution that passes this test: *This solution will enable me to get consistent, acceptable results through my staff.*

➤ Negotiate acceptance of the solution from the persons who are directly involved in the conflict.

➤ Follow up: Did the solution actually work? Did the solution stay in place? If not, go through each step again.

Working with Other Departments and Work Groups (p. 84)

➤ Develop a "big picture" view that goes beyond the scope of the work your staff performs by understanding as much as you can about the overall process and your role in it. Be aware of any special factors or circumstances that can significantly affect your staff and others.

➤ Plan your work thoroughly and make your plans available to others. Notice any changes or developments elsewhere that might affect your plan.

➤ Listen and communicate—to your staff; to other supervisors; to your supervisor; to outsiders you work with.

➤ Think of yourself as a "team member" with other supervisors—with your own supervisor as the "supervisor" of that "team." Then do your best to make this team as effective as you expect your staff to be.

➤ Make your standards and limits known so other supervisors and work groups understand the guidelines that affect the way your staff works. Likewise, understand their standards, limits, and guidelines.

➤ Use other supervisors as a resource—and be a resource to them—for solving problems; for ideas on better ways to do the work; for information that might affect your plans.

Keeping Your Supervisor Happy (p. 85-86)

➤ Know what is expected of you, and do your best to meet those expectations.

➤ Make sure that every goal you set is consistent with the goals of your company or organization.

➤ Keep your supervisor informed; share all the news—good and bad.

➤ Think ahead and plan ahead. Do not let surprises occur.

➤ Be an effective team member.

Resolving Mistakes (p. 87-88)

➤ Be honest; there are reasons and there are excuses, and your staff is smart enough to know the difference.

➤ Talk—one-on-one—with the other person(s) involved.

➤ Acknowledge that you made a mistake, and apologize in an appropriate way. If further action is necessary to "set things right," take that action ASAP.

➤ Remind yourself about what you did that caused the problem so you are less likely to repeat this mistake.

Pulling Together (p. 91-92)

➤ Maintain a sense of purpose; keep everyone focused on the performance results the *team* wants to achieve.

➤ Encourage everyone's involvement in the "game plan" for the day, the week, the month.

➤ Seek a commitment to first-rate performance from each staff member.

➤ Make it easier for staff members to motivate themselves by creating an organized work space where all resources needed to achieve results are on hand and available.

➤ Move quickly and assertively to remove any factor that is de-motivating.

➤ Ensure that team members take good care of themselves and avoid injury or burnout.

➤ Help staff members to improve their individual skills and to develop their role within the team.

➤ Provide support and encouragement for every team member, even when a person's short-term individual performance is not up to expectations.

➤ See that the *team* is rewarded as a group, even if special recognition is given to one or two people for unusually good individual performance.

A P P E N D I X

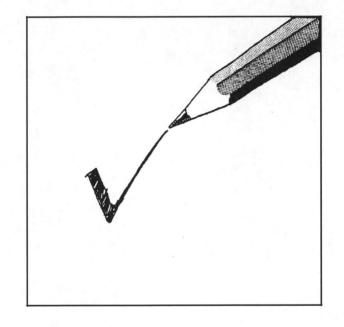

ACTION IDEAS

Idea #	From Page #	*Check here when you transfer an idea to your "Action Plan"* →	

ACTION PLAN

Action Items	Date: _____ Check here when you transfer an Action Item to your "To Do" List or Weekly Goals	
1.		
2.		
3.		
4.		
5.		
6.		

Checklist for Description of Action Items: *name; description of action; expected start date; expected finish date; resources required (current & new); expected effect on performance; how results will be measured; reference to Action Idea #s.*

Authors' Comments on Case Studies

Case #1: Who Will Succeed? (pages 17-18)

Both Joe and Maria will probably survive, but the edge is with Maria. Joe will probably be better liked as a supervisor. But Maria will probably earn more respect. Joe may be too casual about learning the many useful techniques and principles every supervisor should learn; he needs to understand that his promotion to supervisor is just the beginning of becoming an effective supervisor.

Case #2: Which Strategy Would You Use? (page 41)

Strategy #2 looks best, but it is important to also follow up the group meeting with one-on-one meetings to avoid any misunderstandings and improve individual relationships. Angela should not expect 100% compliance to her new standards right off the bat. She must set her standards high enough, however, to raise both customer service and teller accuracy to satisfactory levels. Reachable new standards are required, but she needs to give her staff reasonable time to reach them. While everyone works toward the new goals, Angela should be sure to set a good example in every aspect of her work.

Case #3: "The Kid" (page 45)

Even without experience, The Kid would have performed much better had he realized that he would be rated on what his department accomplished more than what he could do himself. Specifically, he should have focused on planning the work, giving clear instructions, coaching and communicating with his staff, and making sure the work flow was smooth and the work was first-rate in every way.

"The Kid" was lucky; not everyone gets a second chance. One of the goals of this book is to help you get ready for a wide variety of supervisory situations so your chance for success is good—the first time!

Case #4: Sylvia, the Coach (page 49)

Do not wait! Meet with Kevin first thing Wednesday morning. The way Kevin starts is like a "first impression"—it lasts—and Sylvia will not get a second chance. Most people approach a new job with a good attitude and a little uncertainty, and it may be demotivating to be "parked" for two days. Even if it makes her day more complicated, Sylvia should meet Wednesday morning. And she should hold her calls, turn off her cell phone, and give this meeting her full attention.

New-employee orientation is one of your best opportunities for coaching—a chance to touch all four bases: (1) to establish your authority and communicate your standards and limits, (2) to start someone off in a way that makes the person a contributor to your staff's success, (3) to set the stage for future coaching and counseling, and (4) to show that you are the leader and you lead with confidence. You do not want a new employee to get this information piecemeal or from others.

Sylvia should cover the department's goals, the performance criteria she tracks, important procedures everyone is expected to follow, quality specs everyone must maintain, any relevant safety information, special departmental "rhythms" or cycles, and housekeeping matters if they are not covered by an employee manual. And she should establish that she is a good listener.

Case #5: Will MRT Counseling Work? (page 52)

If both Kathy and George make a serious effort to deliver the "rewards" the other wants and they have agreed on, the chances are good that their relationship will improve. At the least, communication between them has been opened up, though Kathy must understand that if she fails to follow through on her side of it, she will actually make the situation worse. Note that each has asked for one "technical reward" (#1) and two "behavioral rewards." In a situation like this, delivering a "behavioral reward" is often more important than delivering a "technical reward." In fact, it is not uncommon for someone to hold back some on a "technical reward" until expected "behavioral rewards" have been received.

The initiative lies with Kathy—even if she delivers all of her "rewards" first and has to prod George to keep his side of the deal.

MRT counseling frequently works because it opens up communication and both parties accept that there is something specific each can do to improve the situation. Supervisors must always take care to exclude from the discussion any reward over which they have no control.

Case #6: Between a Rock and a Hard Place (page 86)

Charlie has two situations to handle here: He has to square up things with Fred, and he has to square up things with his crew. He must deal with both situations ASAP.

Charlie's message to Fred should include three parts: (1) explain the facts; (2) stick up for his crew by making sure that Fred knows he can count on his crew to do first-rate work, even in Charlie's absence; and (3) encourage Fred to stop by sometime during the day and recognize the outstanding work that Charlie's crew accomplished last week—by saying something positive directly to them.

Charlie's message to his crew should also include three parts: (1) Admit that he chewed on them before he knew the facts and apologize for jumping to a wrong conclusion, (2) recognize the productivity they achieved and praise them for the extra effort they made in his absence, and (3) make sure his crew knows he has explained the facts to Fred and stood up for their excellent performance.

It makes no difference which situation Charlie handles first—Fred or the crew. It is important, however, that he deliver all three parts of each message. And Charlie should probably expect his crew to be distracted, annoyed, angry—and unproductive until he has talked with them.

Additional Reading

Blanchard, Ken and Spencer Johnson. *The One-Minute Manager*. NY: Berkley Publishing Group, 1983.

Brounstein, Marty. *Handling the Difficult Employee*. Menlo Park, CA: Crisp Publications, 1993.

Chapman, Elwood N. and Wil McKnight. *Attitude: Your Most Priceless Possession, Fourth Edition*. Menlo Park, CA: Crisp Publications, 2002.

Chapman, Elwood N. and Barb Wingfield. *Winning at Human Relations, Revised Edition*. Menlo Park, CA: Crisp Publications, 2003.

Conlow, Rick. *Excellence in Supervision*. Menlo Park, CA: Crisp Publications, 2001.

Covey, Stephen. *The 7 Habits of Highly Effective People*. NY: Simon & Schuster, 1990.

Fisher, Roger and William Ury. *Getting to Yes*. NY: Penguin Putnam Inc., 1991.

Hathaway, Patti. *Giving and Receiving Feedback, Revised Edition*. Menlo Park, CA: Crisp Publications, 1998.

Haynes, Marion E. *Effective Meeting Skills, Revised Edition*. Menlo Park, CA: Crisp Publications, 1997.

Lloyd, Sam R. *Accountability*. Menlo Park, CA: Crisp Publications, 2002.

Lloyd, Sam R. *Developing Positive Assertiveness, Third Edition*. Menlo Park, CA: Crisp Publications, 2002.

Maddux, Robert B. *Delegating for Results, Revised Edition*. Menlo Park, CA: Crisp Publications, 1998.

Maddux, Robert B. *Effective Performance Appraisals, Fourth Edition*. Menlo Park, CA: Crisp Publications, 2000.

Maddux, Robert B. and Barb Wingfield. *Team Building, Fourth Edition*. Menlo Park, CA: Crisp Publications, 2003.

McEwan, Barbara, Edward Krauss, and Forrest Gathercoal. *On Being the Boss*. Menlo Park, CA: Crisp Publications, 1995.

Minor, Marianne. *Coaching and Counseling, Third Edition*. Menlo Park, CA: Crisp Publications, 2002.

Peters, Tom and Bob Waterman. *In Search of Excellence*. NY: Warner Books, 1988.

Rouillard, Larrie A. *Goals and Goal Setting, Third Edition.* Menlo Park, CA: Crisp Publications, 2003.

Scott, Dru. *Customer Satisfaction, Third Edition.* Menlo Park, CA: Crisp Publications, 2000.

Visconti, Ron and Richard Stiller. *Rightful Termination.* Menlo Park, CA: Crisp Publications, 1994.

Wingfield, Barb and Janice Berry. *Retaining Your Employees.* Menlo Park, CA: Crisp Publications, 2001.

Zemke, Ron. *Working with Jerks.* NY: Simon & Schuster Sound Ideas, 1988. Audiocassette.

NOTES

Now Available From

Books•Videos•CD-ROMs•Computer-Based Training Products

If you enjoyed this book, we have great news for you.
There are over 200 books available in the *Fifty-Minute™ Series*.
To request a free full-line catalog, contact your local distributor or

Crisp Learning
1200 Hamilton Court
Menlo Park, CA 94025
1-800-442-7477
www.crisplearning.com

Subject Areas Include:

Management
Human Resources
Communication Skills
Personal Development
Marketing/Sales
Organizational Development
Customer Service/Quality
Computer Skills
Small Business and Entrepreneurship
Adult Literacy and Learning
Life Planning and Retirement

CRISP WORLDWIDE DISTRIBUTION

English language books are distributed worldwide. Major international distributors include:

ASIA/PACIFIC

Australia/New Zealand: In Learning, PO Box 1051, Springwood QLD, Brisbane, Australia 4127 Tel: 61-7-3-841-2286, Facsimile: 61-7-3-841-1580 ATTN: Messrs. Richard/Robert Gordon

Hong Kong/Mainland China: Crisp Learning Solutions, 18/F Honest Motors Building 9-11 Leighton Road, Causeway Bay, Hong Kong Tel: 852-2915-7119, Facsimile: 852-2865-2815 ATTN: Ms. Grace Lee

Indonesia: Pt Lutan Edukasi, Citra Graha, 7th Floor, Suite 701A, Jl. Jend. Gato Subroto Kav. 35-36, Jakarta 12950 Indonesia Tel: 62-21-527-9060/527-9061 Facsimile: 62-21-527-9062 ATTN: Mr. Suwardi Luis

Japan: Phoenix Associates, Believe Mita Bldg., 8th Floor 3-43-16 Shiba, Minato-ku, Tokyo 105-0014, Japan Tel: 81-3-5427-6231, Facsimile: 81-3-5427-6232 ATTN: Mr. Peter Owans

Malaysia, Philippines, Singapore: Epsys Pte Ltd., 540 Sims Avenue #04-01, Sims Avenue Centre, 387603, Singapore Tel: 65-747-1964, Facsimile: 65-747-0162 ATTN: Mr. Jack Chin

CANADA

Crisp Learning Canada, 60 Briarwood Avenue, Mississauga, ON L5G 3N6 Canada Tel: 905-274-5678, Facsimile: 905-278-2801 ATTN: Mr. Steve Connolly

EUROPEAN UNION

England: Flex Learning Media, Ltd., 9-15 Hitchin Street, Baldock, Hertfordshire, SG7 6AL, England Tel: 44-1-46-289-6000, Facsimile: 44-1-46-289-2417 ATTN: Mr. David Willetts

INDIA

Multi-Media HRD, Pvt. Ltd., National House, Floor 1, 6 Tulloch Road, Appolo Bunder, Bombay, India 400-039 Tel: 91-22-204-2281, Facsimile: 91-22-283-6478 ATTN: Messrs. Ajay Aggarwal/ C.L. Aggarwal

SOUTH AMERICA

Mexico: Grupo Editorial Iberoamerica, Nebraska 199, Col. Napoles, 03810 Mexico, D.F. Tel: 525-523-0994, Facsimile: 525-543-1173 ATTN: Señor Nicholas Grepe

SOUTH AFRICA

Corporate: Learning Resources, PO Box 2806, Parklands, Johannesburg 2121, South Africa, Tel: 27-21-531-2923, Facsimile: 27-21-531-2944 ATTN: Mr. Ricky Robinson

MIDDLE EAST

Edutech Middle East, L.L.C., PO Box 52334, Dubai U.A.E. Tel: 971-4-359-1222, Facsimile: 971-4-359-6500 ATTN: Mr. A.S.F. Karim